Making Things Better

O | R | S Oxford Ritual Studies

Series Editors
Ronald Grimes
Ute Hüsken, University of Oslo
Eric Venbrux, Radboud University Nijmegen

Making Things Better

A Workbook on Ritual, Cultural Values, and Environmental Behavior

A. DAVID NAPIER

Oxford University Press is a department of the University of Oxford.
It furthers the University's objective of excellence in research, scholarship,
and education by publishing worldwide.

Oxford   New York
Auckland   Cape Town   Dar es Salaam   Hong Kong   Karachi
Kuala Lumpur   Madrid   Melbourne   Mexico City   Nairobi
New Delhi   Shanghai   Taipei   Toronto

With offices in
Argentina   Austria   Brazil   Chile   Czech Republic   France   Greece
Guatemala   Hungary   Italy   Japan   Poland   Portugal   Singapore
South Korea   Switzerland   Thailand   Turkey   Ukraine   Vietnam

Oxford is a registered trademark of Oxford University Press
in the UK and certain other countries.

Published in the United States of America by
Oxford University Press
198 Madison Avenue, New York, NY 10016

Library of Congress Cataloging-in-Publication Data
Napier, A. David.
Making things better : a workbook on ritual, cultural values, and environmental behavior /
A. David Napier.
pages cm
Includes bibliographical references and index.
ISBN 978-0-19-996936-4 (pbk. : alk. paper)—ISBN 978-0-19-996935-7 (hardcover :
alk. paper) 1. Material culture–Social aspects.   2. Exchange–Social aspects.   I. Title.
GN406.N37 2013
306—dc23
2013012869

For
Anna-Maria

"I shall never rest until I know that all my ideas are derived, not from hearsay or force of habit, but from my real living contact with the things themselves. From my earliest youth this has been my ambition and my torment.[1]"

—GOETHE, *Italian Journey (1816–17),* entry for 27 June 1787

CONTENTS

The notion that a *thing* could be the focus of an act of thinking has been pondered over since humans began to record their thoughts in writing, and a subject already well-known in ancient Greek philosophy. A thing in its simplest form is an object, something we are able to identify and distinguish from everything else because it has certain characteristics we perceive as external. Every day we apprehend the things around us and come to conclusions about their nature, autonomy, and relatedness to us and to one another. And how we relate to things in turn tells us if we are philosophers, natural scientists, accountants, or builders; because every form of specialization has its own ways of defining reality, existence, knowledge, and so forth, just as every individual who participates in a collective has his or her unique perceptions.

As we commit to particular ways of perceiving the world we privilege various kinds of explanation. We believe that one mode is more truthful than another, and we develop skills that advance our understanding, and that facilitate the decisions and choices we make in life. The philosopher may rely upon the accountant to determine what taxes are owed, while thinking the accountant's concerns mundane; while the accountant may find the philosopher ignorant about life and out of touch with the world. Those who write may think of things as objects, concepts, or figures of speech; while those who build may privilege wood and nails, speaking from time to time, but perhaps not considering speech itself as an object.

Indeed, once we commit to one way of considering things, it becomes increasingly difficult to entertain the others. A philosopher may be contented on occasion to speculate about what a Martian might think of humanity, while living in smug ignorance of a builder's knowledge, let alone a builder from a culture characterized by its own range of ideas and values about, say, the properties of wood and how different woods respond to humidity. One merely has to observe how a philosopher spends his or her days to see that there may be little opportunity to appreciate the values of the journeyman laborer. Though this is a book written to encourage new thinking, it is not a book about philosophy or the history of ideas, and it therefore must reduce its use of a huge body of literature to a few lines and even fewer pages.

To understand, however, some of the fundamental principles this *Workbook* builds upon, and to make the most of its *Exercises* and *Practica*, it is worth reconsidering the dominant idea that the Enlightenment—the so-called Age of Reason in the 17th and 18th centuries—principally gave intellectual force to the separation of soul, body, and experience. The Enlightenment perhaps did this very well; but it also humbly acknowledged something that more subjective forms of philosophy (and especially those called *phenomenological*) tend to discount: this being less that there are limits to perception, than that there may be important *things* beyond what we are capable of knowing completely. Though we have been conditioned to think of the Age of Reason as a villainous form of Euro-centrism, we should not be so evangelical that we forget a central achievement. While philosophers have always pondered the limits of what can be known, it took Immanuel Kant to recognize that *subjectivity* would always have a logical *weakness*: for him, to say that "I can only know what is made available to my sensate mind" is not to say that there is nothing beyond sensation but to acknowledge that whatever may exist beyond that is something we cannot know in a complete manner.

There is a choice to be made, in other words, between staying at home in my mind with the knowledge that I can only know what I perceive and feel, and believing that the borders between myself and the unknown are filled with creative potential. What Kant recognized was that deciding between these outlooks was both a choice and a commitment, and like many explorers Kant made his decision: the unknowable but ultimate character of a thing Kant named the "thing-in-itself" (*Ding an sich*), and he opposed it to the sensational apprehensions of things that would become the focus of phenomenology from Hegel onward.

In this subtle but most profound realization of Kant, we see also not only the limitations of the Enlightenment and its separation of body and mind but also a positive and hopeful domain full of possibilities: the *noumenon* (a thing existing outside of the senses) was to be understood as potentially transcendent and, in part, as a thing existing beyond an individual's sensory capabilities. Kant knew, in other words, that the truly most profound existential question was less whether knowledge could be independent of human sensation and more whether we could ever accept the limitations of cognition itself.

Here, we see why Kant was truly our first anthropologist and why he is the first philosopher to take anthropology seriously. In fact, in Kant's formulation the questions of anthropology reign higher than those of philosophy, ethics, or religion; for the awareness of how paradigms frame our limitations is at the core of his most famous epistemological question: "What can I know?"[1]

Without treading the well-worn path of asking what Kant may or may not have thought about the relationship between *noumenon* and his view of the thing-in-itself, what is more relevant is his active awareness of the limitations of conscious knowledge—a kind of necessary humility that requires us to see the quite radical scope of Kant's anthropology—at once participating in the Enlightenment and also seeing its serious limitations.

Had Kant been an experienced ethnographer, he may have taken the next cognitive step very seriously: anthropology provides us with many examples of cultures in which moral obligation centers less on individuation than on one's responsibility to bring to life primordial things that would otherwise remain unknowable—to acknowledge that we may never fully know things-in-themselves but that we nonetheless accept their critical importance in allowing us to try making things better.

In Balinese culture, rituals must be performed to stabilize not only the Balinese world but also your world and mine. Likewise, much of Navajo ritual is dedicated to bringing back to life in ever new form primordial things that otherwise lie as dormant and lifeless as a virus without its life-giving cell. In both cultures it is critical that humans attend to the question of "What can I know?" and to do so fully aware that I can never actually know completely those very primordial things—be they genes, archetypes, or karmic states—that shape the foundation on which a "me" will be created. Things-in-themselves not only are made by me but also make me. This is why what can't be known must be explored, even if it can never be made fully available to individual cognition—why it is important to attend to the things we may actually never know fully. This is also why we have rituals—those moments of heightened meaning when we bring together powerfully external perceptions that, because they cannot be fully known, appear to us symbolic.

Indeed, two hundred years after Kant, C. G. Jung said much the same about archetypes. They are external and primordial—less perceptual, more conceptual—accessed through a steady and humble exploration of what we can never capture completely. For Jung, as for Kant, for the Balinese, and for the Navajo, this commitment through ritual and symbol is not a defeatist's recognition of our limitations, but an optimist's acceptance of limitless possibility.

While openly acknowledging our limitations demands a level of faith in transcendence (because now there are important dimensions to life that cannot be evidenced directly), such an active acknowledgment of our boundaries is, paradoxically, also part of what makes our actions more real. At first this appears contradictory: how can accepting the existence of what we may evidence only obliquely be a part of what we claim to be real?

The answer is actually quite simple: while accepting our personal limitations can lead us into existential isolation, it can also lead us to look outwardly for evidence of what we may not know—to look for constructive versions of what remains ambiguous and beyond our grasp. In a good way, our very limitations can become catalysts for attending to our spiritual (and artistic and poetic) needs by encouraging us to focus on what seems external to us and can only be known partially. Here, that is, we see how and why rituals are essential for growth; for rituals are not only repetitive forms of behavior but also repeated attempts at attending to the things we might embody but cannot know possessively. Rituals are, in this way, creative forms of what psychologists call deindividuation, forms of behavior through which we attempt in a constructive manner to transcend modes of thought that sometimes place too much unhealthy emphasis on self-knowledge or that drive us to believe that self-knowledge is only an internalized inwardly-focused activity.

Artists also feel this need even if they are unable to transcend the solipsistic identities that define them. Centuries after Kant, Pablo Picasso criticized Cubism precisely on these grounds, remarking that Cubist artists—who had once worked anonymously in search of shared ideals—eventually gave in to the culture of extreme individualism that they inhabited, demystifying what was unknowable in favor of celebrating each individual's environmental impressions. It was not that Picasso did not acknowledge the scope of the unknown but that he felt defeated by what prioritizing individual perceptions had wrought. There were no rules or measure, no norm, no deindividuated ritual obligations—just each person claiming his or her own view, a place of tragic individualism (the suffering artist epitomized by the alienated Vincent van Gogh or Albert Camus's *The Stranger*). Many Cubists, in fact, later went back and signed once anonymously presented works, having given up, Picasso claimed, on their search for what remained mysteriously unknowable.

There is an important lesson here: if we feel defeated by what we may never know completely, we may well retreat, spiraling into isolated, subjective, and ever more internalized behaviors. But if we gladly accept these limitations, there is always the possibility that our interest in what we cannot know might well create a space for something new.

For Picasso, the question of whether a person's relationship to a thing could actually be reconceived remained forsaken and unaddressed once artists gave priority to tired, and what now seem anthropologically quite naïve, notions of identity. In the defeat of metaphysical freedom—by critics, by individualism, and by the self-promotion of artistic identity—we witnessed how art could not change and has not changed in the least since the radical experimenting of the Cubists, Dadaists, and only somewhat more rational Surrealists. Art museums may invite us to explore what we do not know, but today they also focus so much on the fixed identities of artists that they can work directly against feeding our creative needs.

This book is by contrast a kind of painting of something unknown, or at least an exploration of something partially unknowable. It asks us to consider what might happen if philosophers stopped only talking and writing and became for a time builders, ethnographers, or athletes. As a series of experimental actions, it represents a modest attempt at addressing Kant's anthropological questions—not in the form of intellectual rumination but as embodied practice, a merging of the thing-in-itself with the phenomenal perception of things—a kind of ritual deep play that, if nothing more, potentially alerts us to what we may not know.

Because its brief set of experiments evolved as a teaching tool over some thirty years in both undergraduate and graduate courses in ritual, in symbolic anthropology, and in the anthropology of religion, I cannot say that it possesses the coherence of a book written in a fury of passion or in the youthful voice of one who feels the certainty of a kind of moral knowledge just discovered. Because I migrated from art to philosophy and then from philosophy to anthropology, I also cannot claim that what I offer is at all timely in any of these fields. I merely claim that I have given this path no specific name, except as it has been variously defined and redefined for me by the hundreds of students to whom I have offered the same challenges I present herein.

While *Making Things Better* is not directly about anthropology, there is a substantial literature in anthropology that has inspired it. In fact, anthropology has always been concerned with such subjects as economic exchange (Appadurai; Godelier) embodiment and giving (Strathern, Weiner) and material culture (MacClancy, Miller). This book, however, is not about theories of materiality or exchange. Nor is it about theories of agency (Gell, Makarius), or theories of religion and place (Smith 1987; 2004), or the broad and growing interest amongst philosophers in anthropology and alternate modes of thought.

While I applaud and am indebted to so many of these wonderful lines of thinking and in no way dismiss them, the focus of *Making Things Better* is not theoretical. Rather it is an exploration of the embodied practices that many of these anthropologists and students of religion have considered and that Mauss and Lévi-Strauss in particular examined structurally. While *Making Things Better* perhaps, then, owes most to the philosophical reflections of these two theorists, it asks the reader less to think about diverse forms of embodied imagination than to embody other imaginative forms as a technique for understanding particular kinds of environmental commitment.

Whatever weaknesses this book may possess (and I am sure there are many), I trust the reader will not include among them my desire that its writing or publication be either timely or well timed. However, what time has done is make it quite impossible for me to thank all of the people who have contributed to the book's making. In the three decades over which it evolved, countless responses have moved its writing and content, and four parts (the beginning of Chapter 1 ["Autoeroticism"], Chapters 2 and 3, and a section the Epilogue ["No More Einsteins"])[2] were previously published in different unrevised form and responded to by a host of readers.

I cannot at all, therefore, ever hope to thank so many people, except perhaps (if they are inclined to read this version) by later acknowledging whatever memories the reading of *Making Things Better* may evoke in them. Though this invitation may well be a poor excuse for not offering just acknowledgment where deserved, I confess that being so blessed with friends makes me also somewhat more vulnerable to hubris.

Still, there are some, living and deceased, whose names it would be remiss of me not to acknowledge: some for posed initial questions to me as a child and later as a student that became catalysts for writing; others read various versions of the workbook over the years; still others responded directly to its content once formulated.

This catalytic group includes many people: the late Gregory Bateson, Hedda Berntsen, Rosemary Coombe, the late Bruce Dakowski, the late Erik Erikson, Robert Gardner, the late Clifford Geertz, the late Gerard Holmens, the late Jiří Kolář, the late Constant Lambrecht, Miriam Lambrecht, Donald Lopez, the late (and "other directed") Margaret MacFarland, Kira Muratova, Elizabeth Napier, the late Rodney Needham, David Nugent, the late Daryl Posey, the late Benjamin Spock, I Gusti Madé Sutjaja, Crispin Tickell, the late Annette Weiner, and Reginald Young (aka "Terminator 24"). Here, a special note of thanks also goes to Angela Hobart for supporting me during the final revision period at the Centro Incontri Umani, Ascona, Switzerland, where the manuscript was revised throughout 2011–2012, and to my children, Andrew and Harriet, for allowing me to revisit my childhood through theirs.

The editorial respondents (those who actually read and responded to parts of the text) include Jonathan Benthall, Louis Berger, Robert Borofsky, Marcus Colchester, Hubert Decleer (as in "nothing to declare"), Rebecca Empson, Erica Farmer, Martin Holbraad, Roland Littlewood, Jeremy MacClancy, George Marcus, Lee Miller, Robert Muller, Donald Pollock, Margaret Rosenberg, Barbara Tedlock, and Dennis Tedlock.

Those who have worked in both of the aforementioned capacities (as personal catalysts and as respondents to all or parts of the manuscript) include Michael Adelberg, Paul Dionne, Francis Huxley, Pauline Spampinato Napier (my mother), the late Anthony Napier (my father), Anthony Stevens, Paul Stoller, and my wife, Anna-Maria Volkmann Napier, to whom the publication of this volume is dedicated.

With so many wonderful and illustrious respondents I can apologize only by saying that I have not been as good as I might have been in taking on-board their various comments and suggestions. A book so thoughtfully responded to should be better; I have done what I can, and the imperfections are of my own making. I do hope, though, that there are some useful passages here for those readers who are kind enough to risk engaging what follows. You have my admiration, my gratitude, and my condolences!

Making Things Better

INTRODUCTION

MAKING THINGS BETTER EVOLVED over the years out of an expressed desire on the part of students to grasp how modes of thought, and in particular cosmological beliefs, affect the ways we give meaning to experience as embodied practice. It is an honor to be able to publish this workbook in Oxford's Ritual Studies series, and it is a credit to the editorial board that its members recognized immediately the challenge that I am trying to set for the reader: namely, to bring to consciousness the connection between how we place ourselves in our physical environments and how we try to make meaning of that placement through ritual.

In fact, the connection has been central to our understanding of spiritual experience. High-order monotheists—Christians, Jews, Muslims—have over the ages defined religious experience largely in transcendental terms, as have most Buddhists: for this reason monotheism also fostered the world's great proselytizing religions. In each, the afterlife exists both as a focal point of religious achievement and as a constant reminder that where we are and how we consider the things around us mean less than what transcendence holds in store for us. The world stands as largely illusory. Experience can enhance spiritual achievement, but spirituality more often than not remains in opposition to physical sensation, except where physical sensations become elements of ritual, meditative practice, or religious ecstasy.

Such baseline transcendental beliefs are essential to any religion that has universal aspirations and especially those that rely on some omniscient, monotheistic entity (i.e., God). It is also no accident that related modes of salvation stand somewhat uncomfortably against orthodoxy when the spiritual becomes local. From Patristic times Christians have persecuted heretics who have made the Lord's spirituality too earthly. Though I attempted to assess this separation anthropologically some time ago (Napier 1986), saying and doing are not the same: the question of how we might appreciate another mode of thought, in other words, is largely mitigated by various behavioral taboos and prohibitions that are culturally, socially, and religiously driven (e.g., Sax et al. 2010). Thomas Csordas (1994, 2002), for instance, finds that while "charismatic Christians" create extraordinary forms of embodied practice in church services, they invalidate forms of mystical embodiment (e.g., dreams) that occur outside of church-sponsored rituals. Ronald Finucane, in a remarkable assessment of the daily practices of medieval Christian pilgrims (1977), describes the Catholic Church's own uncertainty regarding sacred shrines built to honor saints whose very local displays threaten the Church's universalist aims. And Ronald Grimes, the editor of this Oxford series, points specifically to the problems that arise when the violation of an indigenous spirituality of place must be addressed through laws and policies derived from Eurocentric epistemologies (e.g., Grimes 1986, 2000, 2004, 2006).

There is today an enormous literature on ritual and performance that crosses and unites the fields of religion, legal studies, and history. In anthropology, ritual has for more than a century focused principally on the study of rites of passage (from van Gennep to Leach, Turner, and beyond) and on the understanding of ideological diversity. This book is not about these literatures; however, what follows does depend on them. And though it cannot in any way pretend to examine critically the many contributions made in such a broad field of inquiry, *Making Things Better* does ask that we reconsider a few basic questions that the field of ritual studies has held on to doggedly in spite of the ideological homogenization that global processes promote. Indeed, the very ongoing dialectical relationship between the diverse fields that concern themselves with spiritual practice attests dramatically to the importance of ritual studies in the understanding of environmental behavior.

Where global priorities have suppressed the veracity of experiential differences, the field of religious studies has returned repeatedly to acknowledge them. And while many contemporary anthropologists are uneasy with the fact that ritually generated embodied practices may not always be accessible across cultures or to the lived experience of the ethnographer, religious studies is more happy to consider such differences, even if other fields (law and economics, for instance) must live uncomfortably with them, as the literature on cultural repatriation makes clear time and again. Cultures rarely like how other cultures treat exported artifacts.

As for anthropology, it has not always been so reticent as it may today appear in acknowledging the possible incommensurability of diverse forms of religious experience: van Gennep (1909), Durkheim (1912), and Mauss (1923) all long ago recognized how body image and body image boundary could shift dramatically across ways of thinking and categories of thought. Indeed, Durkheim's separation of psychology from sociology was in part an outcome of his ambivalence about how culture both advances and limits different forms of experience. Already in this early work we see a tension between acknowledging difference and claiming that our capacity to understand a society's functional attributes is universal.

But an emphasis on ideology and structural difference reached its zenith, in fact, among those who studied other religious forms in the field. While Lévy-Bruhl (1910, 1922, 1927) took a less ethnographically informed philosophical approach to the study of modes of thought, fieldworkers such as Malinowski (1922) and especially Leenhardt (1970 [1942], 1979 [1947]) were uncompromising in their descriptions of other ways of thinking as incommensurable with Cartesian, monotheistic categories. Leenhardt was especially adept at exploring the implications of cosmology for body image. As a Protestant missionary to New Caledonia, he redefined the meaning of sustained, long-term fieldwork, spending nearly forty years researching the relationship between Christian ideology and indigenous categories of thought.

Such structural and functional concerns were also elaborated in North American anthropology, especially in the writings of Whorf (published posthumously in 1956) and Hallowell (1955). Whorf's (and Sapir's) argument that the structure of language affects us cognitively, and Hallowell's interests in what today would be called the phenomenology of embodied practice, allowed for ritual studies and anthropology to merge more fluidly than perhaps ever before.

However, without doubt, the study of the relationship between cognitive and cosmological difference comes together most dramatically in the structural anthropology of Lévi-Strauss and his followers and critics, such as Douglas (1966), Leach (1969, 1970), Turner (especially his later, and also his posthumously published, work on performance [1975, 1988, 2001]), and my Oxford supervisor, Rodney Needham (1972), who not only was a major critic of Lévi-Strauss but, through his translations, also responsible for introducing Lévi-Strauss to the English-speaking world.

Needham would famously ask of his students why philosophers should spend so much time imagining what visitors from other galaxies might make of human behavior when there were still so many diverse ways of thinking in the world—indeed, as many as there are language systems at work, if only we might take the time to learn how indigenous categories function at the level of human behavior. And while the study of alternative ways of thinking lived on in such magisterial ethnographic works as Godfrey Lienhardt's *Divinity and Experience* (1961) and also in a range of new ethnographies of religion, such as Danforth's (1989) and Kapferer's (1997) studies of spiritual embodiment, much of anthropology moved toward a more reflexive consideration of how anthropologists accessed others, spoke for them, and represented them as accessible, leaving anthropology's contribution to such debates over the role of language in cognition to critics of psychology, such as Berger (2006).

So, why, we may ask, has the responsibility for examining what is less accessible shifted to some extent out of anthropology and not only into religion and law but also into indigenous studies itself (e.g., Sioui 1992)? In part, the answer is obvious: while anthropologists increasingly devote themselves to the belief that the lived experiences of those we study are accessible and can be represented through the giving of voice to others, the acknowledgment of the mysteries of religious experience inveighs against any easy translation.

This is why today religious and ritual studies have taken a lead in addressing directly the relation of perception to experience; it is also why not only ritual studies but also performance studies (e.g., Schechner 1993), human geography (e.g., Tuan 1974; Tuan and Tuan 2001), praxis research (Bourdieu, de Certeau), and the fine arts (Koerner; see, e.g., Latour and Weibel 2002) have emerged as the meeting place for the theoretical examination of alternative modes of thinking about embodiment (e.g., Bell 2009a, 2009b; Grimes 2008; McDannell 1998; Morgan 2012; Smith 1987; Stephenson 2010). Indeed, the broad range of themes covered by the journal *Material Religion* illustrates just how wholeheartedly these problems have been embraced. In a recent volume of that journal (7(1), 2011), for instance, we find precisely this kind of cross-disciplinary research—combining Latour's focus on fact as fetish (the *factish*), an assessment of ritual studies (Grimes), and long-standing anthropological work on sensation (Howes 2003, 2005, 2009).While other anthropologists have also contributed significantly to our understanding of the senses as an embodied experiential form (most notably Stoller 1989, 1997; Pink 2009), the study of diverse sensory modes has all but been expelled from much of social anthropology (see, e.g., Napier 1986, 199–206). Is death, for instance, more tragic for one who believes he or she can never return to Earth to make amends than it is for one who believes himself or herself to be eternally reincarnated? One resists judgment of course, but should one also resist learning from the experiment that thinking in this different way makes possible? Such ideological pioneering has always been central to anthropology, even if it now more resides in fields as diverse as phenomenology and experimental psychology—the latter, for instance, where Jung, through his notion of the collective unconscious, was among the few to take seriously Lévy-Bruhl's meditations on shared representations.

Thanks to ritual studies, the profound influence of modes of thinking on human behavior remains not only a living but also a thriving field of inquiry. Do, therefore, forgive the following project if it seems too directed toward a particular way of viewing the world—and do also understand that the way chosen here is only one of many, but one that is enough at odds with post-Enlightenment thought to be challenging in the minds of the students of religion who have trialed the manuscript over the years. Please also, then, be patient and forgiving of yourself if you find engaging this workbook at moments challenging or frustrating. I am aware that there is a fine line between challenging readers and offending them; I certainly hope I have not crossed it.

Preamble to the Workbook
Rights or Rites?

Education is the art of making us ethical.

—HEGEL

Just Remunerations

This book is about how ritualized ideas of what constitutes *the material world* create diverse notions of the meaning of exchange, of reciprocity, and of fair trade. In so doing, it also asks what might comprise a *just remuneration* for things traded or taken. It is, then, not about economics—though its target is in part economic—but about the problem of assessing what constitutes fair compensation in circumstances where indigenous wealth, and especially inalienable wealth, has been taken unfairly from individuals or groups who may neither share the global values most of us assume are universal, nor so readily make a commodity of a world whose wealth is made ritually.

While the book is about indigenous rights, it is not a comprehensive examination of the burgeoning academic literature on the cultural and intellectual property of indigenous peoples. Rather, it is constructed as a workbook of four exercises designed to challenge those who use it by provoking questions about how *value* might be variably established within cultures or local groups that are much at odds with economic trends. It is, therefore, about how unique systems of value challenge us when we attempt exchanges across various cultures and domains of knowledge. And it is about why indigenous groups have been, and so often still are, unfairly remunerated when they trade their heritage or have it stolen.

So, this book is unusual: it takes a number of well-known premises and forms of thought—indeed, forms found and recorded from around the world but discounted in the new global environment—and invites readers to experiment with them through four simple exercises. These exercises are not designed to make readers into, say, polytheists or animists. However, they do facilitate, as they have for many groups I have taught over the years, a limited exploration of various forms of embodied thinking, to the degree that they ask us to question what might constitute fair exchange in systems of value unlike our own.

Because the book explores modes of thought much at odds with global priorities, each exercise is followed by an essay designed to provoke thought about the problems posed in that exercise. In turn, each of the four essays is followed by a practicum in which those who have actively engaged the workbook are invited to apply their perceptions to real problems posed by exchanges across domains of value.

Making Things Better, then, is designed to raise the question of what is a just remuneration—especially within contexts where global forces provoke exchange or engage in the outright theft of indigenous intellectual and material wealth. So often, it seems, advocates for indigenous peoples cry out for fairness to those whose property is taken unfairly. Yet the activities of advocates are nearly always limited to fighting for one right or another, stopping short of asking what remunerations there may be that are different from, greater than, and more important than financial ones. Most of us cannot conceive of what an exchange might be in a case where something taken cannot be valued as a commodity (see, for example, Scheper-Hughes and Wacquant 2002).

As our notions of *fairness* with respect to disempowered local groups are nearly always couched in terms of justice and human rights, it is necessary, first, to ask why pleas to universal human rights, such as those made by countless human rights advocates and advocacy organizations, have thus far failed to have a genuine impact on the plight of indigenous peoples and those who are more generally powerless. To say uniformly that they have failed is to make a strong claim, but who can ignore the irony? While the voices of those who claim to represent the disadvantaged grow louder, other ways of thinking about the world grow the more quiet. Part of this deference by less powerful indigenous peoples to their more powerful global advocates arises from legitimate concerns: powerful global forces—both well- and ill-intentioned—require of indigenous groups that they see themselves in "our" terms (Napier 2003, 119–28). Even where self-determination is a priority, autonomy is always defined as a political aspiration.

What is more, indigenous people who speak out against the tyranny of either their own bullies or the advocates who appropriate their causes are often the first to be victimized by those local tyrants when advocates disappear to their conferences, summits, and awards ceremonies. When I was a health volunteer in Latin America in the late 1960s, I recall that even schoolteachers who attempted to buy farming equipment cooperatively were assassinated for their "socialist" actions as soon as proactive nongovernmental organizations disappeared. Indeed, the very human subjects review committees that oversee research *demand* that we make anonymous, and to that degree erase, those we study. Who, then, demonstrates much care for indigenous systems of value?

But the problem is deeper. If our human rights advocacy is based on the right and proper idea that people around the world deserve the same basic rights, it will do that initiative no good to say that systems of value vary radically from culture to culture; because to focus on difference is to focus on variable, rather than universal, needs and values. To say, for instance, that indigenous groups in Malaysia should not be remunerated for their medicinal knowledge because they do not believe it can be owned is to get dangerously close to saying that we can take that knowledge without remunerating them in any way. Cases abound that demonstrate this tendency not to remunerate fairly: to say that no concept of money or capital exists in a culture or that people suffering from chronic lung disease are happy to exchange an oil concession for a tin roof that doesn't leak is to open the door by which cultural difference is used as an argument for exploitation.

Thus, to argue for any kind of human difference is, for human rights advocates, to open the possibility that those who take will justify not remunerating for what they have taken, especially when local values are not based on making commodities out of cultural, material, or intellectual resources, let alone religious ones. But throwing out cultural difference not only leaves us open to becoming intellectual imperialists—global vigilantes for good or bad—it also robs us of the treasure of knowing how much we have yet to learn about what is humanly possible. How can we know, for instance, what an aboriginal Australian or a Native American is giving up to a mining company unless we can imagine, if faintly, what it means to be tied both spiritually and bodily to a concrete place that is now being mined?

This book will not answer that question, but it will ask the reader to consider it more complexly than do the programs of human rights lobbies or environmental justice movements, because it ask readers themselves also to give something up—namely, the universal hegemony of their own system of value. The ethical dilemma here is not only, then, about treating others fairly on their own terms but also about how we generate curiosity when we do not recognize the depths of our own ignorance. It is this emptiness, this not knowing our own ignorance, that led Hegel to define education as the art of becoming ethical—that moment when we realize our ignorance and attempt to do something about it.

Limits to Human Rights?

When I published my first article on intellectual property and indigenous rights some twenty-five years ago, the literature on the subject was, to say the least, rather thin. Prior to the Rio Earth Summit of 1992, there were occasional pioneer meetings on the subject, a few devoted advocates for indigenous rights (e.g., Marcus Colchester, the late Darrell Posey, members of Survival International and Cultural Survival), and a few rare attempts at drawing up exchange agreements with indigenous groups (some of which we will address later in this book). But there was really no outstanding body of knowledge applied to the question of just remuneration. Indeed, most of the legal precedents came from cultural return cases, and nobody really had any clear idea of how to remunerate a group that was not politically autonomous or incorporated. Today the literature is enormous, including not only legal arguments about possible mechanisms for compensating groups rather than individuals for their local knowledge, but, more pervasively, also arguments about economic justice and the redistribution of worldwide wealth.

Because this growing literature is based on the justified premise that every world citizen deserves much the same opportunity as the next, its goal is to establish common, humane standards by which each and every human being might claim a right of access to a minimal standard of living and a right of protection from unfair exploitation by oppressive global forces. To put it bluntly, the entire human rights enterprise remained somewhat opaque to knowing how to remunerate because the field itself was rightly predicated on the premise that we're not supposed to think of other people as "different." In fact, this is so much the case that many human rights advocates are often downright anticultural, believing that all arguments for cultural difference merely provide excuses for those who wish to use difference as a tool for taking advantage of others. "Oh, aren't all of those poor peasants happy," the tourists say as they drive through local squalor in their air-conditioned buses. "Just look how happy they are with so little."

But if our human rights narratives must, then, of necessity suppress human difference in the interest of providing equal justice, how will we ever be able to provide just compensation for things exchanged or taken when systems of value diverge radically? If we find ourselves discounting outright different, culturally driven modes of thought—different ways of organizing the cosmos—how will we ever learn about the richness of human thought that was once part of the world's intellectual diversity? So, our problem is not only one of asking coldly, who can say what is a just remuneration, it is also one of asking the deeper anthropological question: who can say what others perceive to be a just remuneration, and who can say this in a world that willfully discounts cultural difference?

While much of what follows in this book may be viewed as a challenge to the failures of human rights discourse, I must emphasize that I am not denying its importance. However, I am saying that focusing exclusively on such language absolves us of asking a much harder question—namely, how do we remunerate those who have different value systems if and when we one day get around to attempting genuine compensation of a kind that is more than just financial?

In the meantime, let us not forget that, in the absence of any true dialogue about the diversity of systems of value across cultures, there exists no lack of individuals who, or groups that, will gladly seize the pulpit of self-righteousness indignation in telling us what those without voice need and ought to have. Let us, therefore, not fail to see our own self-promotion in assuming the role of speaking for others who we claim have no voice; because the very audacity of moral gatekeeping can itself as much hinder as help those very disadvantaged individuals we all agree to be so much in need. Before beginning the following thought experiments, then, permit me two notes of caution: one about organizational advocacy and one about individual advocacy.

What Advocacy Organizations Miss

In 1990 Maurice King published a short article in Britain's leading medical journal, *The Lancet*, in which he recommended that charitable funds for oral rehydration therapy in the world's most devastated societies be revoked. King argued that there was no sense in saving infants from death by dehydration only to let them die, as statistically they do, from the greater agonies of infectious diseases and human conflict. The article provoked a huge outrage not only because King was openly advocating withholding aid from the most needy but also because he had been responsible for helping save millions of lives as a chief advocate for oral rehydration.

Not long after the publication of King's article, an international conference was held to debate his argument. At the conference were leading representatives from the world's major charities. In a volume produced following that conference, King expanded his thesis, arguing that societies entering what he called the population mousetrap could not recover with the assistance of foreign aid and that once totally deteriorated they could not recover at all.

But the real trap was less the one described in King's paper than the one walked into by the aid organization leaders who attended and spoke; for the presentations of those present (later published in a single volume) said as much or more about the mission of each organization than they did about King's argument. What most had failed to realize was that King had not only an overt but also a covert target, the latter of which was to demonstrate how, left to their own devices, these organizations would use the event's platform to reify their specific missions. In so doing, they one by one walked into the subtler trap set by King— to show how justifying their existence took priority over cooperation in the field.

These participating organizations, that is, had fallen into a mousetrap of King's own making. The subtext of his initial letter was that if charitable organizations cannot work together in the field, they will almost always work at cross-purposes: meeting their own short-term targets; recruiting away from existing programs (and for high wages) all and any skilled local labor; setting goals that would satisfy funders—in short, placing their own replication ahead of the long-term welfare of the populations they ostensibly served.

While this is not the place to engage the growing literature on the failures of the aid industry, a look at the published document from this conference demonstrated better than any argument how the grandstanding of organizational representatives placed them squarely in the trap set by King. Likewise, James Pfeiffer (2002) found that nongovernmental organizations create not only their own exclusive societies in the places they work but also their own economies—often harming local institutions by hiring away their most professionally qualified employees, and undermining, thereby, already fragile public resources.

But one finds almost no discussion in any of these global initiatives of how restitution can be facilitated in local terms; for international aid itself thrives on the universal sentimentalizing of human tragedy. Not that such a tactic is unjustified, but its bold assertion in nearly every case shows most clearly how universalizing and hegemonic are the structures of these organizations despite their best efforts to claim otherwise. And what then of individual advocates?

Rights or Rites?

The argument thus posed by this book is that if you truly wish to know what another person might desire as compensation for a thing taken unfairly, then first you must sense what ways that person favors for making meaning in the world. Human rights are a fine thing when they can be established and regulated, but they are mere foils for self-promotion if they are not accompanied by some hard work at assessing how just remunerations are understood by those in need, which, in turn, means learning how others make value locally.

If our first goal, then, must be to understand otherness by exploring unknown experiential territory, a more rigorous intellectual program is required. Some say you can never adopt wholly a different way of thinking; but we would not be naturally capable of sensing other possible systems of value and meaning were this entirely the case. That we are capable of sensing the worlds created by other cosmologies and modes of thought is in itself an exciting thing to contemplate—a world where the universal idea of basic rights is complemented by a knowledge of the rites and rituals that allow for deep meaning to be cultivated in another's local moral world (e.g., Kleinman, Das, and Lock 1997). It is with this degree of existential rigor that readers are invited to experience in the following pages a few of the ways deep meaning can be cultivated among those who steadfastly refuse to make commodities of the local worlds they inhabit. In this spirit of exploration, the following workbook has been written. As a one-time homeless friend put it when discussing his plight to a more fortunate audience, "You don't even know what you do not know." Let us, then, even in very small measure, try to sense the vastness of what we may not know.

PART I | Things and People

EXERCISE 1 | Shaping Behavior

If all the things that grow from earth
exist in earth, then earth must be composed of all things
unlike itself that spring from it.
—LUCRETIUS, *The Nature of Things*, Book 1, Lines 867– 869

Step 1

Take an object, preferably an object that is important to you (a memento, an heirloom, some so-called consumer good that you have invested in), and permit yourself before beginning this exercise the luxury of honoring that thing for a moment or two. Do not allow yourself to be concerned immediately about the moral differences between possible choices. Do not, that is, feel guilty that you have been attracted to your new shoes instead of the religious object you inherited from a loving grandparent, or to your bankbook instead of a special ancestral ring, or to some gadget instead of a photograph of Yosemite Valley. Just try to give yourself the freedom of connecting to something and to making that connection as freely as possible; the goal of this exercise is not to demonstrate how difficult it is to suspend moral judgments about material things but to cultivate a level of meaning that many so-called traditional peoples would say has been lost on modernity. So please, do not proceed until you have found such an object and spent enough time with it to feel that this thing could conceivably be more important to you than you had previously imagined.

If after some moments you have so convinced yourself—by religious conviction, self-imposed austerity, or simple frugality—that you cannot allow yourself to be so attached to material things, then instead do what religious healers and diviners have done and yet continue to do in so many non-Western settings: read the omens. Permit yourself, that is, to think that the first thing that spontaneously impresses itself upon you—a leaf, a kitchen utensil, a piece of plastic, an obstruction in your path—has, or soon will have, some reason for being there.

And now, if the task of so doing is still overwhelming, take some time to think about why this exercise might come so naturally to others; think of why you have difficulty engaging in such a silly or foolish challenge—why you resent, or even are angered by, such behavior. Even if the task does come easily, perhaps you may still need to think about why you have always felt it enough just to consider yourself superstitious; for if you cannot get past this initial challenge, you are unlikely to be capable of transcending your private prejudices about material things to see that not all the world lives on divisions such as natural/man-made/organic/artificial or real/imitation. If, that is, you cannot entertain the idea that a soda bottle can be as much a part of your symbolic world as a leaf of grass, you will not fare well in trying to sense how members of other cultures who appear to be wholly attached to their so-called landscapes have managed to make such deep attachments to the physical environments they inhabit.

If you continue to find this activity troubling, then perhaps you can tell me what keeps so many indigenous peoples tied thoroughly to the practice of making spiritual the things of this world. If—especially if—you identify yourself as an environmentalist or consider yourself frugal, you may have extra work here; because the idea of loving a physical thing often does not come easily for the puritanically inclined, even though it may be the single sentiment required in understanding why other cultures have fared more successfully than yours and mine in loving the world that each of us locally inhabits.

So please, before continuing to read this book, do actually engage in the experiment. Do not imagine only what it might be like within some made-up, idealized fantasy or some literary or poetic contrivance to have your objective world be other than it is. For if you fit the object you have chosen into only your imagined moral world, you will merely have demonstrated to yourself that you are, indeed, unwilling to embody any new view of what *things* actually are or may be. This imagining, I argue, is true both for the iconophile (those who love icons, and, hence, this experiment) and the iconoclast (those for whom materializations of the spiritual are idolatrous); it is as true for the nature lover (who believes humans have wreaked havoc on the world) as for the ascetic (who sees the world as illusory and will not let material things carry any good meaning). It is true for the gluttonous consumer (who just wants everything) as much as for the capitalist (who believes that everything has its price).

The point here is that if you agree to dirty your hands a bit before continuing to read, you will have a somewhat different view of what objects can mean. Artists, for instance, accept the notion that works of art are catalysts for all manner of imaginative thinking; however, artists also know that the works they create are (at least traditionally) physical things that must be lugged about and that may deteriorate over time or be destroyed if neglected. Their works are not, for the most part, only mental artifacts.

Step 2

This awareness of materiality is why, after you have selected an object, you should be with it in space and time, doing your best to imagine that it is the locus of something extraordinary. You may identify this extraordinary thing as a sentiment; you may call it a power; you may wish to personify it by calling it spiritual. But, regardless of your inclination, the importance of the exercise is to mark this object as something of merit, something worth caring about. The object should be understood as something, therefore, very different from any other object, even one that appears otherwise identical to the object you have chosen. Your object should be uniquely connected to you both empathically and emotionally. You need to develop, in other words, some deep feeling for it.

So if you find yourself having difficulty engaging in this experiment—if, for example, you have been acculturated to think that having a fetish or behaving in an animistic fashion is retrograde—please stay with the task. Things will change. Besides, you owe it to much of the rest of the world to give it a go.

Step 3

Now, attend to your object at least once a day, and perhaps several times a day, over the coming week. Try to understand how it functions and what you can do to improve your relationship with it—how you might enhance its meaning or your own actions and reactions to it. Try to be especially aware of how its new meaning influences your behavior—how the so-called environment becomes a very different place when you have located special meaning in a particular thing that inhabits a particular space. Does this new system of belief make you aware of how your object has become integrated into your behavior—into why you go to particular places, into how you decide to go there, into what happens when you return, into how you return to the setting, the place, inhabited by your chosen object?

At the same time, start a journal in which you record the impact that your new belief system is having on your behavior. Note how your behavioral patterns—including the details of your everyday actions—have been specifically influenced by your object and your beliefs about it.

Here, it is necessary to make sure that you attend to the hard work of seeing the exercise through. Not only can the initial entertainment of the novel experience give way to a bond that is demanding or even frightening, but also, as your involvement builds and possibly even destabilizes your old world, every cultural mechanism that has kept you from this activity in the past will present itself now with increased force. As you finally begin to sense better what, for instance, a Native American might actually mean by having an "attachment to the land," your commitment will be tried repeatedly by conventions of all sorts.

If, for instance, you are a good capitalist, you will feel that you are now at a disadvantage for investing yourself in something that cannot be exchanged easily, that cannot be taken or given up on a whim. If you are a good Christian (or Jew or Muslim—i.e., a monotheist), you will feel that it is an offense to

God's omniscience to require material connections for spiritual satisfaction. If you are an environmentalist, you will feel guilty if your object is not natural and especially if you have randomly selected as your object some industrial byproduct; you will be troubled to know that traditional peoples—and especially good animists—can bring spiritual meaning even to modern plastic appliances. If you are aesthetically inclined or an artist, you may find that you are disturbed by the ease with which the tasteful world you inhabit can have less meaning than all of those pedestrian things you once so readily dismissed. And if you are a psychologist or one thought to be in good mental health, you will be angered by what you take to be regressive behavior and especially by having agreed to engage in an activity you were meant to have grown out of long ago. You will say that healthy psychological development depends on being able to distinguish yourself from things in your environment and on social skills acquired after early childhood. You may even feel that the very thought of this exercise is unhealthy or taboo or even that it should be prohibited in the interest of mental well-being.

You will, in other words, by all manner of cultural prejudice be tested deeply in this phase of your exercise, and you will ask yourself repeatedly if this is not something that you should give up as quickly as possible. You may even claim to be bored as a strategy for distancing yourself from this way of looking at things, even if you may also now acknowledge that it could be a characteristic feature of so much of non-Western, or "non-global," living. But try to hold out for just a bit longer, because I promise that this initial task is almost fulfilled.

Step 4

Now, after a week or so of attending to your object, take it to the trash and try throwing it away. Try, as we say, to recycle it. Try telling yourself that it is just a material object and that it can be replaced. Try convincing yourself that it is not good to be so attached to or obsessed by a thing—that you are morally a better person for not needing the material world at all—that materialists are psychologically immature. Try to make any argument you can for abandoning this thing.

And if you can manage to distance yourself from this thing, see what happens when you put it out of your life—in a drawer, in a room you never enter. Could you give it to a friend? On what terms might you do so? What would you expect in return were someone to accept it? Would you tell them its story? Would their use of it add to its merit? Would the circumstances surrounding your object grow beyond your idea of it? Would it begin at some level to have a life of its own? Imagine what it might be like to sustain this relationship for a lifetime or in a family over several generations. Imagine if you had an ancient origin myth that had its basis in the object relation you have now created. Finally, were you to find a way of giving or exchanging your object with another person, ask yourself under what circumstances you might be in a position to get it back.

Having completed this experiment, you are now ready to take any otherwise meaningless object in your environment and attach to it a special meaning that cuts across your earlier prejudices about things and about which things matter. Now that you have come this far, take something really common and work with it—something ubiquitous in modern life, something you live with every day. Let's say a car, for instance, for part of the argument of this book is that if you can't create a symbolic relationship with a car or some other common feature of your everyday existence then you are unlikely to understand why an indigenous person might sell off his rice fields for a chance at owning the very thing you yourself might profess to hate.

CHAPTER 1 | Meaning and Property

1. Autoeroticism

Animating an object (enhancing the power of something we already value or finding a thing we can connect to in such a way) requires lots of imagination and persistence. In fact, most of us will find it easier to attribute such forms of attachment to other places, other pastimes, or other exotic peoples. So it is best to forego these more serious tendencies by taking a lighter approach, by thinking about things everyday and ubiquitous—like maybe your car. "A car," you say? "Only true materialists and flagrant consumers get attached to cars!"

Well, permit me to be more direct here—to be more challenging without (hopefully!) alienating you as reader. Think about it: if so many indigenous peoples thrive on creating local meaning through an embodied animation of things and local landscapes, ought we not also to do the same if we wish to understand how others get attached to the places they live in? How can we profess to know what another is trying to do if we cannot also sense what that person expects to happen?

For anthropologists who devote entire careers to the study of both the habits and the artifacts of other cultures, the absence of car talk in societies wherein hundreds of millions of these rolling, invasive, sometimes derelict or abandoned objects proliferate is astonishing. It brings home just how immunologic is the era in which we now live—how, that is, we separate so much of our everyday world as not-self and not of us; how rejection of the realities of modern life results in the kind of environmental paradox whereby what we profess as meaningful and what we engage in experientially diverge strikingly.

By this I do not mean that we talk about fuel economy while driving a Porsche or massive SUV. What I mean is that the disjunction between what we claim to value and how we spend our time is far greater than it is for cultures in which individuals are encouraged to take more seriously the relationship between what they are and what they consume. We even go so far as to invent hideous neologisms to recommend this sorry state: the concept of *quality time*, for instance, stands, paradoxically, as an obvious sign of the extent to which our daily lives are characterized by activities that we do not value and, therefore, cannot understand. And on the environmental level—where energy consumption more or less becomes the measure of behavioral correctness—we wholeheartedly engage in activities like fighting for the preservation of areas of outstanding natural beauty while our real lives remain characterized by the perpetuation of the junk process. The nature lover in the characterless compact should be pitied for his or her loss of self, not admired for the pseudo-frugality of what is meant to pass for an environmental statement about not needing a fancy car. Today, dissociation is not only intellectually rationalized but also sometimes morally upright.

These were the sorts of thoughts running through my head when I read in the *New York Times* some years ago a brief review of *Wild Wheels*, Harrod Blank's quirky documentary about those who take a more personal and active role in the remanufacture of their daily transport. What attracted me to the review was a belief that I have held for some time: the effects of treating a common thing (say, a car) as a fetish are, in the long-term, far more ecologically sound than the behavior I regularly see exhibited by my friends and academic colleagues who have never experienced a single blister or greasy hand—those who drive morally correct vehicles (about which they know nothing) for limited periods of time and then just as morally dispose of them for the next politically correct piece of mobile modesty. What makes them any different from the aristocrat of old whose status was measured by the tenderness of his fingers?

Sure, the kind of personalization of a car—the animation—we see in *Wild Wheels* seems odd to the self-conscious, politically correct cosmopolitan, the one who finds it perfectly acceptable to live without knowledge of how all of that metal, plastic, and petroleum byproduct actually functions to provide a mode of transport. Yet the very romantic poets we admire so much regularly made and continue to make the effort to celebrate the lives of those who live close to experience, who have some tactile appreciation of where they are. And just where are *we* when we now define the environment as eternally out there, beyond the realities of the fingers that clutch those weird rolling things we must sit in, avoid, insure, repair, and finance?

Wild Wheels is, in my view at least, probably an inappropriate title for a film that concerns itself with cars that have been highly personalized, cars that, indeed, reflect an owner's commitment to the responsibilities that ownership of a physical thing should entail. In this film people make cars out of wrought iron in response to dreams; they glue buttons, or postcards, or mirrors, or rubbish onto every inch of their vehicles in an attempt to bond—like some traditional healer—with a primary factor of their lived experience. Seeing this film makes a viewer in the least become concerned with the real contradiction between the stated objectives of our so-called environmentalists and the frequent inability of such individuals to define the environment as a place in which they actually live. A thinking person becomes concerned, moreover, at how their political correctness itself perpetuates consumption—whether the demand for expensive, disposable economy cars isn't part of an industrial ploy to get us to buy them more often and use them more regularly. Odd that we should assume that driving one is irreproachable; for what do we mean by ecologically sound? In Blank's film, nearly every bizarre relationship between a person and a car is bound by two beliefs: the first is that the car is an unavoidable part of modern life; and the second is that bonding with an object you or I can rarely avoid makes us care for the thing itself and for how it is used. These people have all, in other words, fully embraced some version of Exercise 1.

Though our romantic poets would never have gotten near a junkyard, those who drive "wild wheels" are actually reminding us of the concerns that gave rise to the rustic inclinations of our romantic forbears: now we must stand back while the proprietors of these roadside eyesores step forward as traditional leaders in what is now called *recycling technology*. And they're right, for so much of our clap trap about being responsible consumers is relative: imagine a nation of agriculturalists, most of whom could not describe the workings of a harrow or plow. We (and I include myself here) run the old Toyota into the ground, get rid if it, and then turn around and wax Wordsworthian about how a Native American of long ago became absolutely tied to his or her respective teepee. Sure, the economy car gets great gas mileage, but how many mountains of ore actually go into creating all of those new cars that we drive to excess and with such a sense of self-righteousness? And just how many cars have you spotted in your latest Sierra Club calendar?

But nobody in *Wild Wheels* would think of disposing of their cars—at least not without a proper burial ("my Cosmic Ray Car died on me...so I'm burying it"). One woman spends thousands to rebuild a highly decorated, but very tired, Toyota sedan ("when my Art Car breaks down, I feel like there's a part of me that's not sewed on, like my whole image is crumbling"), while another man deliberately chooses to remodel a 1960 Cadillac because it stands for all of the opulent sins of American life ("I specifically selected a 1960 Cadillac because it represented the height of American opulence...an [overstated] caricature of American society").

Meanwhile, the rest of us labor with the uncertainty of "choosing" the proper statement. Do you, for instance, buy that Toyota because its operating costs are cheapest over the brief life of its sheet metal? Do you buy the diesel because it gets great mileage even though it fills the air with particulates? Do you buy the Saab because its emissions are so clean that running the engine in a closed garage (deliberately or not) won't even give you a headache? Do you buy the Honda because it's made in America? Or, now that health-care talk is trendy, do you buy the Jaguar because (yes, a survey has proven it!) this car will keep more of us out of emergency rooms than any Mercedes or Volvo? Well, there's a politically correct motive for having any of them, but let us not forget that the recycled old banger (despite its poor gas mileage) will certainly require less excision of all of those new resources that the mining companies have now found beneath the South American rain forests.

Indeed, I would argue that the cars of the past—like the obsessive objects of Blank's film—are the real cars of the future. Not only do they have the least impact on un-mined resources; the more time you devote to the privileges they provide, the more it hurts when someone drives into them. And, because they frequently do not work, they will never encourage the dependence that a new Honda does. In addition, they provide gainful employment for those caretakers (mechanics) who help us develop more meaningful relationships with our vehicles. If they one day become real classics, we may then find them spending more time in pieces on garage floors (while we accustom ourselves to public transport) than they will on any highway.

2. Behaving Industriously

So how then do we rewrite a revised *Workbook on Environmental Behavior*? Well, let's start out afresh. First of all, stop reading *Consumer Reports* before you buy a car. Like American relationships, which on average last around 1.5 years, all of their data are based on short-term relationships. Instead, try finding something you can establish a deep sympathy with. Yes, you may one day find yourself recycling a "classic" hand-built car—where appreciation truly means driving less—but you may also find that any old car can have a personality once you have decided to take responsibility for your decision to own it. Stop denying your participation in this over one billion strong phenomenon. I, too, hope that we will soon have no cars on our roads; meanwhile, get a grip on that very large old steering wheel!

Now, once you have reached this wonderfully free space, you can consider yourself liberated from at least one ancient and long-standing cultural prejudice. OK, I now own the frequently inoperable 1969 Buick sedan; what do I do with it? Well, take it for a meaningful ride, spend some quality time with it ("I don't take this car to the grocery store on a daily basis, so it generally is a very different experience"); think about where you are going and whether you really want to go there badly enough to risk a ride in the old beast.

Learn to live with its eccentricities, and try to forget about the horror stories associated in the past with owning such a jalopy. Recognize its imperfections. As the great Baroque sculptor Bernini put it, take the imperfection itself and develop it into a thing of aesthetic merit: "make use of a defect in such a way that if it had not existed one would have to invent it" (Baldinucci 1682 [in Napier 1992, 125]). "If you think you're not getting your art seen," states one woman in the film who has placed plastic fruit in the smashed grille of her station wagon, "do like I do—make your art on your car.... I want a strong reaction, and I get [that] in the streets, because I'm dealing with people who never go to art galleries. They have a...fresher attitude."

With such challenges before us, let those who are most truly creative get more involved with that older automobile; for a car is an eternally imperfect thing. It is no wonder, therefore, that the Japanese—who as a culture are fascinated by the presentation of immaculate gifts—have not focused on the longevity of the steel itself. A simple scratch spoils the virginity of the object. So put aside the new, and choose a car with a character to be tamed. Something like the Gremlin, for instance. Remember it? Who could forget such a memorable experience? In a tribute to the greatest lemons of all time, the *Wall Street Journal* offered the perfect eulogy:

Design critics complained that this car looked as if it had been rear-ended while on the showroom floor. The manufacturer advertised it as "pure and simply more fun to drive," but the Gremlin was so cramped that when passengers swung the front seat forward to get in back, the horn honked. The engine tended to conk out inexplicably on right turns. Seats were covered in vinyl so slick that the driver slid away from the steering wheel going around a corner. The windshield-wiper knob was right by the light switch and looked about the same—a hazard at night or in a rainstorm. New: $2000. Now: $150, negotiable (*Wall Street Journal*, December 1, 1989, 1 [in Napier 1994: 672]).

At least one Gremlin, in fact, looms colorfully in Blank's film—covered from end to end with what looks like dyed pasta. Indeed, many of the highly personalized cars he shows are the rather nasty, expendable things that are almost never thought desirable—as if owners of such junk feel compelled to make a special effort to convince themselves and the world that their personal investment in money and human agony is "worth" something. Perhaps it is our memory of a cynical and opportunistic Detroit that keeps these vehicles out of the parking lots of trendy shops and that makes it so easy for us to buy things new and "foreign"—like a millenialist looking for a spaceship or an environmentalist searching out the experience of some beautiful place made more meaningful by the absence of other members of the species. It's hard, the same journalist reminds us, for most people to forgive these unlovable motoring atrocities when, as with the Chevrolet Corvair, one's own rear wheel could be a real menace on a sharp turn, "pinch[ing] the tire, deflating it and sending the car into a spin or flip" (ibid.).

But Blank shows us other, more constructive ways to develop a fetish into "an eclectic statement." As one young man who grows grass on cars puts it: "there's a whole process the car goes through, from the time it sprouts until it dies." Then there's the "5:04 Special," named for the exact moment when a California earthquake dropped a brick wall on it and left it transformed though perfectly functional. (It's even got a vanity plate!) And nobody will forget the gentleman who uses a pointer to escort viewers through the diorama of Seattle, Washington, that he has constructed on the roof of his car. Here we not only experience, as it were, "Japan in a dishpan," but also are provided with a meta-critical lecture on urban vandalism: "buildings in this area," he shows us with his pointer, "were stolen; this building was deliberately removed from the car and placed under the rear tire."

Throughout this film we have example after example of how people have taken this major part of all of our lives and treated it as if it were a major part of all of our lives. Sure, none of us really likes having to hang out in traffic while reading William Wordsworth, but there are solutions. David Best, the creator of a number of well-known decorated cars, puts it aptly:

> My approach to the automobile is to fight it. When I work on a car, I redesign it....Anything that's next to my hand goes onto the car. If there's a dead rat, I'll grab it and glue it onto the car....A piece of plastic is [as] natural to me and as [much a] part of our planet as a rock is....We have to stop the idea of hating one object over another. That's what perpetuates the junk process, the plastic process. The waste of our society is that people think, well, this is disposable. Nothing is disposable. We don't throw rocks away and we shouldn't throw plastic [or cars] away [either].

Odd though this perspective may sound to wholesome yuppies or self-conscious environmentalists, let us not forget the kinds of meaning that can be created when people allow themselves to take real responsibility for the things we have made. And let us remember that members of some cultures really do try to take better care of the physical world and the unlike things, as Lucretius said, that spring from it.

If you don't believe this to be so, take an exotic holiday. Moments after arriving in Bali, for instance, you will enter a taxi bound for your much anticipated hotel paradise. It is your first experience outside of Bali's international airport, and it can be unusual: the taxi itself may be a Japanese or Korean micro-something, but even today it may still be a 100+ square foot 1960s beast from General Motors—dumped on Indonesia years ago and still alive. Though a surprising if not disorienting object, the time-warped car is not, in fact, what attracts your lasting attention so much as a smell of incense that leads your eye to flowers placed neatly on the dash—an offering to the vehicle's spirit.

Yes, though we may be reticent about admitting it, a car in Bali, like any other object, will always be something of a fetish—that nasty label, wielded like an accusation by splenetic Freudians and Marxists and even by self-abnegating Protestant Buddhists. It's much easier, isn't it, to dismiss those people who get involved with such unforgiving objects—certainly much easier (though, by Balinese standards, more dangerous) than trying to understand and be responsible for the specific "Thing" (not the *kind* of thing) any of us drives? And for those who think that the pages of a little book about a serious topic should not be devoted to such trivia, let us not forget that getting one's own house in order is the first requisite of hosting a guest. Being serious about what we do, in other words, is less a function of taking on the trendy big issues in modern life (or of reading all of the important books or of being global) than it is of knowing how to push a broom—one that, if the skill is mastered, can also double as a paintbrush.

What, then, is true ecologically is, as the Balinese show of the old Chevrolet, also true of aesthetics. "Everything I put on that car," states Larry Fuente, a Cadillac aficionado featured in the film, "has a personal significance to me...either its color, its shape, its cultural significance....Every object that's glued or applied to the car is an art object itself." On any grounds, a car should be chosen only for its attractiveness—its ability to sustain the responsive attention of its owner. If, therefore, you must drive it, please do it meaningfully. "When I get in my car," states one individual with a steaming boar's head protruding from the grille of his aging Ford Falcon, "it's a whole different deal."

So, do try to think of your car as meaningful; and if after so trying the idea of loving a car is still too much for you then maybe you should go to cable TV and watch a car program. Watch, say, *Monster Garage*, where people devote themselves to making bizarre moving vehicles. Or go to an auto parts store and buy a cheap video about hot rods. Why not, in other words, try creating concrete meaning in the concrete world that most of us truly inhabit?

Remember, the things you may choose to animate are being selected by you not because they suit your tastes but because they are specific devices for tying your memory to where you are right now. It is therefore important, if any of us is ever to sense how notions of property are culturally constructed, to stop discriminating among different kinds of things. Don't tell yourself that you have to find, say, a colored leaf or a special stone before you allow your immediate environment to impress itself upon you. If a leaf happens to present itself, then well and good; but to see how local attachments function in other cosmologies it will do no good to limit your horizons to those things that conform neatly to your current prejudices.

That's why in a book about ritual, indigenous rights, and cultural property we are beginning with cars rather than with Sierra Club landscapes; for once you take the matter seriously, you will be better positioned to realize how so-called environmental responsibility is largely divided into meaningful things we treasure and meaningless ones we would as soon consume and recycle. This form of environmental discrimination, in other words, is not merely a function of personal taste or choice; it is something that is very much written into a long-standing tradition we have inherited by which we think of spiritual things as largely not of this Earth and of material things as distractions from the spiritual.

Ultimately, these two tendencies result not only in particular, culturally driven ideas about what is property. They also create behaviors that dissuade us from coming to terms with other forms of spirituality that are readily evident in many, less globally focused cultural and ritual settings.

3. What Is Property?

By *property* we commonly mean those things that are owned or can be possessed by individuals or groups of people united by family, nation, or economic affiliation. At the same time, we now recognize that any definition of property is easily challenged when we transcend our own cultural prejudices. Property is, of course, largely composed of material things, but its definition is also influenced by attitudes about what moves the world (i.e., by cosmology) and by the degree to which those thoughts and attitudes can themselves be owned. Property, therefore, may also include forms of knowledge, as in intellectual property. Ownership rights to this latter type of property are recognized and protected by patent, trademark, and copyright law. Objects and other forms of material wealth are also protected as personal property, while land ownership rights are recognized under the laws of real property.

In this small book we will try to show how different views of property are very much dependent on how readily various cultures can separate people from things. "Divide and conquer" you might say—even if the phrase is used with an entirely different intent here. Obviously, the things that are easily separated from people can also be most easily viewed as commodities, whereas the things that are hardest to separate ourselves from are the most difficult to make into commodities by attaching to them a monetary value (heirlooms, for instance). Because in many societies the distinction between people and things is not hard and fast, we need, on one hand, to experiment with various ways of relating to objects; but we also need to look more closely at why those who would even put a price on everything cultural (economists now love to talk about cultural capital, after all) find other forms of relating to objects problematic.

Though this book is not meant to be a commentary on capitalism (at least not primarily), it is nonetheless worthwhile reminding ourselves that capitalism works best when everything has a known price—that is, when any thing can be exchanged for any other thing or things. And of course this is a condition most easily achieved when people refuse to develop complex spiritual relationships with the things that surround them.

In fact, much of Euro-American economic philosophy, regardless of political orientation, has focused on cultivating this refusal to spiritualize the material world: good capitalists have always used money to make more money (in fact, this more or less defines capitalism), and good socialists have argued against the evils of materialism. Most Euro-American religions as well have inveighed against liking "things" too much. So whether we are talking about Karl Marx or Adam Smith, the common ideological thread of Western economic thinking is that Sigmund Freud was right to believe that the elevation of an object into a fetish was a bad thing. To wit, consider the first and second biblical commandments that the Catholic Church melded elegantly into one: "Thou shalt not make strange gods before me."

What this book instead intends to show is that much of the world did not and does not think this way—that in fact even the most generous of us have probably helped perpetuate the misled notion that to want a material thing is greedy and that greed is the primary cause of one group's taking advantage of another. Sure, this is an enormous problem; but seeing inequality across cultures only as a moral question—and the remedy only at the level of human rights—has positioned us to react to human tragedy much in the manner of a racing dog on a track: we chase the rabbit but fail to recognize that its speed is elsewhere controlled. We may, in other words, think that fair trade or charity will redress an inequality of material wealth, but we are duly embarrassed when those we give to turn around and want the same kinds of material things we cannot resist ourselves.

Likewise, our tendency to couch every global inequality in ethical terms fails to attend to something much simpler—namely, how our rules of what constitutes property and ownership unfairly disadvantage those who view the material world differently. I'm not just speaking here about the problem of relocating someone from ancestral soils to make way for one or another development project; I am talking about how our very concept of an *owner* unfairly disadvantages others.

We, for instance, hear every day about the unfair treatment of indigenous peoples, but how often do we hear about how defining who can be an owner excludes groups who have not incorporated—that is, who have not become a collective legal individual? Where are such discussions taking place? Certainly not on the pages of most newspapers. At the same time, knowing what it means to own something tells us what can be called not only property but also an owner.

Oddly, this problem is seen most clearly not in laws relating to titles and deeds (in land tenure disputes, for instance), but in copyright, trademark, or patent law. This is so because in the case of intellectual property the need to define who owns an idea requires some discussion not only of who is the legal person who owns a piece of physical property, but also of what, in fact, it means to be an idea holder and how this legal person owns a specific idea. The concept of legal personhood also explains why a business also needs to be incorporated, to become a corpus or body—to be a legal person. It is why the Supreme Court in the last century determined that to own intellectual property it would be necessary to classify a collection of people (company employees, for instance) as a *person* (Marchand 1998).

I realize that I am getting ahead of my argument a bit here, but once you think about what making a business a legal person does for that business's abilities to own knowledge, you will also realize why it is essential to talk about intellectual property rather than about property generally, or only about concepts like *ethics* or *justice*. As long as some incorporated groups of people have personal rights normally restricted to individuals, while other unincorporated groups don't, there can *never* be, to use another cliché, a level playing field. So let us take a moment to talk a bit about intellectual property.

4. Property and its Protection

As the age of salvage ethnography gives way to another characterized by the absence of untouched tribal groups, the need to combine ethnographic experience with some awareness of the legal consequences of publicizing various forms of indigenous knowledge becomes evident. Indeed, few anthropologists realize that their own writing—the intellectual candor through which tribal knowledge enters the public domain—may actually be the very thing that denies tribal peoples their cultural and intellectual property rights. Copyright, like trademark, protects the *way* knowledge is presented. But through the act of publishing, the underlying tribal knowledge about which the author has written becomes available to the public and widely disbursed. This availability, in turn, may make the knowledge itself less or not protectable as an indigenous group's intellectual property.

Moreover, even when intentions are clear, let us not forget that the legal issues of intellectual and cultural property are still much disputed within the cosmopolitan world itself (e.g., Brownlie 1992; Coombe 1993; Moustakas 1989; Posey 1990). Students of these subjects cannot readily dismiss the profound lack of agreement concerning how best to protect rights to inalienable property: the reluctance, for example, of nations that regularly import cultural property (e.g., Japan, Switzerland, West Germany, Britain) to support the United Nations Educational, Scientific and Cultural Organization (UNESCO) Convention (on the Means of Prohibiting and Preventing the Illicit Import, Export and Transfer of Ownership of Cultural Property) or the long-standing refusal of the United States (until 1988) to join what has been called "the premier instrument of international copyright" (Benko 1987: 6), the Berne Convention, illustrate this lack of agreement.

And that is only part of the problem: despite the fact that membership in the World Intellectual Property Organization is open to any member of the Paris or Berne union or any member of the United Nations, the age of technology transfer has enabled disgruntled business partners to exploit quite dramatically their independence and noncompliance for financial gain; because leniency offered by a noncompliant country attracts capital. What follows, then, is an ethnographic view of intellectual property with special reference to the patent rights of indigenous peoples.

The irony of establishing what is meant by the term *intellectual property* is that at least one common understanding of what property means is subverted by the contemporary understanding of what is at issue when human knowledge is at stake. Merriam-Webster's Dictionary, for instance, defines as property not only a thing or things (such as land or movable goods) that are owned by someone but also "something that one has the right to use" (as when "the contribution of one scientist becomes the property of scientists to follow"). In this section, then, I will argue that the successful repayment for having utilized the intellectual property of indigenous peoples will occur (if it can at all) less through attempts to apply existing national laws and international agreements to indigenous peoples than through the fostering of long-term personal relations among concerned indigenous and nonindigenous individuals or groups.

If a respect for difference may be said to be the first rule of diplomacy, then the appropriateness of any intellectual category for negotiating across cultures may in a similar spirit be quickly determined by assessing its capacity to help resolve actual problems and to isolate the conditions under which such categories are ineffectual. Like psychoanalytic categories (which may or may not be valid across cultures), those intellectual categories that function most successfully in more than one cultural setting do so not because they force diverse experiences into existing categorical frameworks, but because they help us recognize where and how actual phenomena deviate—where understanding the discrepancy between the category and the event it is meant to define actually results in a better assessment of what is at issue.

If, in other words, the intellectual property rights of indigenous peoples are to be preserved, we need to hone the concept of intellectual property into something rigorous and to do so by whatever trials best indicate its current limitations. Though advertising a new drug may depend on reiterating all of the occasions on which its efficacies and dangers have been demonstrated, assessing its range of applications can be done only by examining its potential effectiveness under new or novel conditions.

While the flow of ideas from one individual to another may be controlled in a number of ways, modern nation-states agree that patent protection is the single most important vehicle through which intellectual property rights may be secured. To assess what may be at stake for an indigenous group possessing a marketable commodity (say, an herb or other natural product having medicinal value), we must first then determine what kinds of intellectual property are patentable—not because copyrights and patents are the only means of protecting intellectual property, but because they are the primary means by which indigenous property is appropriated for financial gain.

Identifying patentable property is in itself no easy task, particularly in the international context. As a start, we must first accept the ineffectuality of any existing international agreement. As a rule, the more international the scope, the less powerful the legislation. No agreements can be legislated universally, and none of them can provide any real protection for indigenous groups, which, by definition, are not usually independent from the nations in whose boundaries they reside. Second, we must come to terms with the universal tendency to employ national laws (which vary enormously), as if they had, or should have, international authority. Because of the ineffectiveness of international law, its inapplicability to indigenous groups, and the tendency to assume that national habits ought to be embraced universally, looking at international protective agreements is far less productive in assessing how humans actually come to respect indigenous intellectual property than is examining what kinds of activities—ritual or otherwise—bind people morally. Indeed, coming to grips with a local moral world may be the single most important way the anthropological method differs in its approach to problems of intellectual property from those legal or political methods that rely on international agreements that almost wholly bypass indigenous groups. If we know personally what others mean by property, we are better positioned to understand what they may expect in exchanging it.

Employing a set of guidelines provided for presumably ethical principal investigators at a major research university yields some useful generalities about how the citizens of more litigious states (researchers, policymakers, and corporate representatives) might actually respond to an indigenous intellectual property claim. These guidelines include the following items as protectable: "(1) a *process*, such as a method of applying a vapor barrier to silicon materials; (2) a *machine*, such as a new instrument to deposit uniform layers of metallic compounds; (3) an *article of manufacture*, such as an assay kit for an infectious disease, or class of diseases; (4) a *composition of matter*, such as a new molecule (characterized by amino acid sequence or base-pairs), or a new chemical compound; (5) *new and useful improvements* of the above; (6) any *distinct and new variety of plant* which is asexually reproduced; (7) any *new, original, and ornamental design* for an article of manufacture"(Harvard University 1988: 43).

5. What Is Intellectual Property?

According to most nationally and internationally accepted standards for determining intellectual ownership, a patent application for a new product must be: (1) *new* or novel— "the invention must be demonstrably different from any existing prior art; this means it cannot be described in prior 'public disclosures,' which include publications and/or availability of the invention to the public, as a commercial product, for example" (Harvard University 1988, 44); (2) it must be *useful*—"the invention must be useful in ways which represent improvements over existing products and/or techniques" (ibid.); and (3) it must be *nonobvious*—"the invention cannot be obvious to a person of 'ordinary skill' in the art; non-obviousness usually is demonstrated by showing that practicing the invention yields surprising, unexpected results" (ibid.). Newness and nonobviousness serve to define what is not in the public domain. Though usefulness or utility is sometimes unclear (as when the scope of a molecule's use is unknown), one's chances for patenting a square wheel will be limited by what seems reasonable as much as by formal law.

What sorts of local cultural conditions are most at risk from these criteria? From a multitude of potential hazards, three areas of cultural concern emerge as critical: (1) the identification of the patentable thing; (2) its ownership; and (3) its causal agent (and, more broadly, its role in an indigenous cosmology).

5.1 Identification of Patent

As the previous conditions make clear, a patent cannot be obtained for a broad class of chemical compounds alone; an agent or agents must be isolable and even the patenting of a single compound will normally not be granted without some specific description of how it has been synthesized and the specific structure of its synthesis.

In the case of protecting an ethnopharmaceutical, we are therefore immediately presented with two related problems. First, it is not enough to know the tree, the shrub, or the animal from which a product is derived to obtain protection. Second, though a process may be patented, the definition of what is necessary and what is contingent is not very broad: though a dog's leg may not actually *prevent* a formula that includes atropine from stimulating the heart, it will not do to include it in applying for a patent or to bring it to a court of law. As the famous biologist Ludwik Fleck once said: "It is easier to find one's way in the woods than in botany. It is also easier to cure a patient than to know what his disease is" (Tauber 1991:64).

Since, therefore, the indigenous cultural description will neither lend itself to chemical specificity nor conform to the procedures of laboratory practice, any discussion of how intellectual property rights can be established and maintained for indigenous peoples will necessarily focus on long-term educational avenues by which these groups may learn the necessary laws to which their property may be subjected in other cultures, or on the custodial goodwill of those who represent them or who function as their advocates. Ideally, such protection would comply with guidelines established by an international body (such as the World Intellectual Property Organization); but in the absence both of an international body with real executive authority and of the requisite time to educate large masses of indigenous peoples about laws that are often at odds with local moral orders, custodial goodwill is essential.

Such goodwill necessarily relies on either the nation in which an indigenous group resides or the ethnobiologist who (or corporate entity that) isolates a particular compound and describes its synthesis. Though the law may be unclear in many ways, what is perfectly clear is that the one who does this is its legal owner and retains for whatever duration the right to sell or license its use. And who is to say, moreover, that the ethnobiologist has not made a discovery if the compound is new; it is useful; it is nonobvious; and it certainly was not known (even though it functioned in many cures) before he isolated it? And if this fieldworker has indeed made a discovery, why shouldn't he or she, too, enjoy legal protection?

To answer this last question, of course, we must first determine if the knowledge actually was his or hers. And what knowledge are we speaking of? Can an individual be said to possess a right to intellectual property if he or she does not possess the intellectual categories to determine the scientifically recognized active agent? Most laws say no, though morality may indicate otherwise. Furthermore, if the biochemical knowledge does not belong to the ethnobiologist, or chemist whose is it?

5.2 Authorship

As the previous discussion illustrates, the problem of identifying what is patentable is directly linked to the problem of ownership—and, by extension, to whether we are dealing with an invention (which is unique) or an innovation (which streamlines an existing art). Can a shaman be said to possess an intellectual property right if he, as the user of a number of substances that include one or more active agents, cannot isolate the active substance in his recipe? Moreover, how can a tribal inventor responsibly subscribe to the transforming of something spiritual into a commodity when, even at major research institutions, "a substantial majority of the faculty are not aware of what constitutes an invention" (Harvard University 1988: 42)?

Those who would wish to find the matter less complex might argue that the relationship between knowledge and ownership is intuitively grasped, that the perception of knowledge as power is a human universal, and that therefore the concept of an intellectual property right is something that should be readily understood by anyone. What is at issue in the case of indigenous property rights, however, is not whether the human mind is capable of producing and controlling powerful information, but whether the indigenous categories that govern this knowledge in any way conform to the cosmopolitan category of intellectual property as a thing that is new, useful, and nonobvious.

Though we might wish to think the issue straightforward, it is not. In fact, without some understanding of the specifics of indigenous life (about such concepts as agency, authority, ownership, and object relations), the practice of regulating intellectual property rights dissolves into empty rhetoric or into unproductive narratives about saving tribal life when what should be discussed are the potential avenues by which individuals may learn enough to stand a chance of negotiating their own entitlement. After all, certain indigenous systems of intellectual property protection (e.g., esoteric magic) actually sensitize practitioners, as we will see, to concepts very much like those that are essential for the successful international protection of intellectual property. The situation, however, is complicated by the fact that, while shamans and other owners of exclusive knowledge in tribal cultures may be said to perform a balancing function in the daily affairs of their neighbors (say, in settling disputes or in presenting requests to the gods), it can hardly be said that they always work in the common interest. To the contrary, their powers may depend, quite directly, on their ability to produce harm as well as good and, through whatever means, to fend off challenges to their authority—a fact that itself may as much be demonstrated through ritual practice as it is evidenced in any written code or law.

If an anthropologist or biochemist has a moral obligation to the indigenous people who have shared with him or her a certain form of knowledge that contains something patentable, how are we to proceed in ascribing intellectual property rights if the relevant knowledge is, for example, held by exclusive inheritance, or if the individual who holds that knowledge is considered a rascal by his more passive neighbors? Part of the problem with international goodwill here is that little of it proceeds from any real understanding of local moral realities; what is worse, a great deal of this goodwill is predicated on the blatantly false assumption that all tribal peoples are egalitarian, that people in these cultures do not suffer from their own despots, and that, if given the choice, they would reject wholesale the bankruptcy and collective corruption of the Western world. At the other end, of course, stand those who are highly cynical about these stereotypes and who argue that we need look only at how goods sent as disaster relief are sometimes mercilessly bartered (for example, by some Third World despots to the Fourth Worlds they victimize or by black market profiteers) to realize how essential locally negotiated reciprocal agreements are for property protection.

These difficulties, however, could (were we critically prepared to examine them) lead to quite different conclusions. Far from providing excuses for custodianship (for saying that *we* have to control *their* intellectual property to distribute fairly whatever benefits it may produce), such problems could also encourage us to rethink the extent to which we are asking others to participate in our own peculiar cultural sagas about saving the world or about lost golden ages populated by noble, fair, and highly individualistic people whose ideas are always new, useful, nonobvious, and fairly shared.

Without digressing at length here, it is important to raise this problem because thinking about our own cultural mythemes leads us to examine, in general, just how unrealistic our salvation dramas about assisting others may be and, in particular, how unlikely are the scenarios we imagine when we think through the implementation of just remunerations for indigenous knowledge. We might even argue that the power of such sagas to influence our collective imagination is such that we are incapable of recognizing the demise of other forms of life until they can be brought to conform to the major plot in which a silent and innocent savage mind is rescued in the hour of its demise by a modern-day Rousseau flying a cargo plane or another such reconnaissance device.

The argument here is not only that we are incapable of controlling the desire to enroll others as straw men in this cultural drama, but also that once the possibility of loss becomes real the actual loss may already have taken place. Teddy Roosevelt embraced the idea of a national park system precisely at the moment when the mapping of the American wilderness had eliminated the true category, and he and J. P. Morgan subsidized the feverish, romantic, and encyclopedic photographing of Native Americans by Edward Curtis at the very moment in history when the eradication of all bellicose forms of otherness in the United States had guaranteed that the swan's song could go unchallenged. If the connection between our greatest and greediest capitalists with an earlier swan's song does not convince us of the need to reassess what is at stake in the current debates over intellectual property rights, then perhaps the growing popularity of such concepts as cultural capital (which, interestingly, was an invention of management specialists) and procedures like social price costing (which addresses our felt need to commodify empathic relations) will alert us to this trend.

Obviously, the goal in this discussion is not to criticize the goodwill that has resulted in development concepts that are frequently unworkable, but to shape the concept of intellectual property into something realistic for indigenous peoples or, failing that, to see it for what it is.

5.3 Agency

Patenting knowledge, as we have seen already, is highly dependent on the notion that property is something exclusively held—by one individual, an institution, or a definable corporate entity—and that what is held is not part of what is shared or obvious to members of society at large or to people outside of the group. In this sense, authorship is synonymous with agency. The difficulty arises when a form of ownership is collective. Things that are shared are generally obvious, and to secure an exclusive right to something patentable an applicant must demonstrate that his or her idea is nonobvious. Shareholders in a corporation are not collectively sharing obvious knowledge but are empowering the corporation to exclude others for its own gain. As long as ownership and agency are synonymous, obviousness is not a problem, but, as soon as a patent begins to look like something already known, exclusive ownership (who owns what) becomes contested.

It is for this reason that "'obviousness' is most frequently cited by patent examiners as the reason an invention is not patentable" (Harvard University 1988: 44). In one sense, tribal shamans would have little difficulty with understanding the nonobvious, since, as we have seen, the nonobvious is usually demonstrated "by showing that practicing the invention yields surprising, unexpected results" (ibid.). For some shamans, this more or less accurately defines what they do. Nonobviousness becomes complex when we marry this concept to the idea that for an invention to be nonobvious it "cannot be obvious to a person of 'ordinary skill' in the art."

Contrary to popular belief, magic—far from being a primitive system of hocus-pocus—actually shares a great deal with contemporary conceptions of how intellectual property is protected, and in particular provides some insight into how inventors actually regulate the use of their ideas in the absence of government interventions. First and foremost, magic is secretive except to those who have negotiated to share such knowledge (the analogy here is, of course, the licensing of patents). Indeed, we might even argue that indigenous priesthoods that control ritual access to sacred magical knowledge bear an eerie resemblance to Western patent-pooling cartels (Suchman 1989: 1285).

Furthermore, there is, in fact, no evidence to support the widely held belief that "the opposite to a publicly structured market for intellectual goods is no market at all" (Suchman 1989: 1290). Secrecy, as much in the West as elsewhere, is a *primary* technique by which intellectual property rights are retained; for within limits secrecy functions well (both for tribal priest and bench scientist) without government intervention. As the president of one innovative computer chip manufacturer put it, "in this business, only the paranoid survive." Remember, we know only what shamans choose to reveal. We also know that we will not learn about their indigenous ethnobotanical knowledge without a deeply cultivated sense of reciprocity, moral engagement, and personal trust. It is here where the greatest challenge resides for both policymakers and ethnographers.

The problem, however, is complicated by the fact that, while the subject matter of international law is extremely rich, cross-cultural comparative work on the legal content of indigenous ideas about property is so rare that "the ratio of empirical demonstration to assumption in this literature is close to zero" (Suchman 1989: 1290). The problem with systems of magic and secrecy—that is, the real reason we very much need legal intervention—is that they promote well-known forms of nonproductive behavior in which rights are so protected that essential knowledge is denied to other potential innovators (ibid.: 1292). Disenfranchised people are often no more willing to discuss their intellectual property with ethnographers than are academics to circulate unpublished manuscripts. They often also do not pass such knowledge on to their own descendants. In such cases, knowledge is simply lost.

Ironically, the problems of securing intellectual property rights arise at the exact moment when indigenous peoples consider their knowledge obvious enough to share openly. Those Arcadian tribal peoples we intend to "save"—that is, not the bellicose ones, but the ones who engage in the peaceful gathering of nuts and berries and the unselfish distribution of common good—are precisely those hunters and gatherers who, social evolutionists tell us, live without cultural specialization and who therefore share knowledge of all tools and survival procedures. These are the generous versions of ourselves that we hold up to the many funhouse mirrors that form the backdrop of our swan's song—for the absence of greed is the thing that for us is, as it were, least obvious. They are also the models of public sharing that, by definition, exempts them from any patent rights.

The unamenability of the concept of intellectual property to that of collective ownership is seen quite clearly, that is, in the difficulty we have in describing what constitutes an ordinary skill in the art in an indigenous setting. It is also seen in the complexities of incorporating indigenous groups that have their own criteria for establishing social boundaries—for determining who we are as a function of who we aren't. Though this is not the place to examine the general issue of how cultural property law has influenced the corporate identity of indigenous groups (e.g., among Native Americans or Australian Aboriginals), it is worth noting that when traditional peoples are forced to negotiate their identities in contemporary legal terms, what takes place is not at all unlike common efforts to redraw municipal boundaries in advance of a local election.

What is far more culturally complex is the issue of assessing what is and what is not an ordinary skill. Is an ordinary skill, for example, the shared knowledge of how a medicinal plant is used? If so, the common knowledge in Guyana that nuts from the greenheart tree can limit fertility does not, at least presently, entitle the indigenous peoples who use greenheart nuts for that purpose to the patent for birth control that could result from the synthesizing of a molecule of greenheart. Nonobvious means what it says—the knowledge cannot be obvious to anyone except its owner. In other words, being moral does not simply involve the general admission that it's their idea and not ours. The concept of tribal egalitarianism itself excludes those very tribal peoples from competing in the patent courts. What they know is commonly shared, and if it's not commonly shared we cannot be party to any squabbling or, to invoke the children's parable, Mr. Gumpy's boat will surely overturn: "Well, might as well secure custodial rights, no? At least *I'm* not greedy."

Such a concern over misplaced ownership would be unwarranted were it not for the fact that even in our well-managed centers of consumption the concept of what is nonobvious remains both the most complex of the three aforementioned requirements and the one most subject to broad and often inexact interpretation:

> For example, it might be argued that a new method of controlling protein production in bacteria is obvious in the face of prior art because it relies on a collection of well-known, existing and proven concepts. Conversely, one could argue the same method is *not* obvious because certain specific elements of the method yield surprising, unexpected results. Judging what is obvious to one of "ordinary skill" in an art is rarely straightforward, especially in technologically complex and rapidly changing fields. (Harvard University 1988: 44).

This problem, finally, is most emphatically seen when the greenheart nut is perceived in Guyana as a gift of God or, more complex still, the gift of the gods in general, who, among themselves, will not or cannot determine who first had the idea of using the nut to control ovulation.

One widely held definition of obvious, then, is "that which is taken for granted." But this definition is also problematic: how, for instance, is a person meant to embody a sense of ownership and self-interest if the knowledge in question is obvious to the degree of being either self-evident or God-given? Our Guyanese native who believes the greenheart tree to grow everywhere and the knowledge of its properties to be self-evident will need to become cosmopolitan very quickly if she is to benefit from any commercial derivative of greenheart. But the very process by which she gains that knowledge may actually limit her claim to the privileges of tradition. In short, she can easily become trapped: as she adopts the behaviors that will allow her to become more familiar with an international commodity exchange, she becomes less traditional, since the negotiation of her intellectual property will require that she redefine a traditional religious framework in terms of a modern system of property. What is more, in making this transition, she not only will become less traditional but also may actually forfeit her claim to the minority rights provided to the disenfranchised.

In conclusion, then, the allocation of rights to indigenous peoples is deeply dependent on coming to terms with whether an indigenous concept of property can be aligned with a dominating legal one. But it is also dependent on indigenous groups recognizing that they will be able to compete on a level field only if they too can gain individual identity for collective behavior—that is, become corporations—legal persons—of one sort or another.

In the meantime, we must move away from the abstract sentimentality that positions indigenous peoples to be subjected to our vague sentimentalities and direct our attentions instead toward concrete empathic relations with others and toward focusing on the specific rules that have unfairly positioned indigenous groups in a global economy. These problems will, in the end, be less remedied by aid programs than by giving others a fair chance in the first place. To achieve fairness, personal involvement in the lives of others is quite obviously essential, and creating moments of heightened moral meaning—ritually or otherwise—becomes imperative.

PRACTICUM 1 | Securing Indigenous Rights

THE FOLLOWING LIST OF suggestions and questions are meant to assist readers in becoming directly involved in the issues raised in Chapter 1.

Readers are invited to review this brief list and to think about ways they might involve themselves in addressing some of the complex issues that must be overcome in creating fair relations between indigenous peoples and those who benefit from their systems of knowledge.

1) Identify an organization that defines itself as a defender of indigenous rights.
2) What is that organization's strategy for defending indigenous rights?
3) Evaluate that strategy's strengths and weaknesses.
4) What could be done to improve that strategy?
5) How might you contribute to that improvement?
6) How might you structure a social networking initiative—say, a website—that would open up the problems you have identified for discussion by other activists?
7) How might you structure such an initiative so that concerned members of the public could lobby for or against organizations that have control over the rights and the futures of indigenous peoples?

EXERCISE 2 | Creating Local Value

Part 1

When you awake tomorrow, dress in a way that for you is completely out of character. If your usual attire is casual, dress in some very different casual style, or dress up completely—tie, jacket, silk dress and heels, whatever, just so long as what you wear and how you present yourself is completely out of character. You may even decide to dress up in one stereotype or another that you think you can successfully define.

1) During that day take careful notes—on how you feel; on how others respond to you; on how you may possibly alter your behavior or presentation of self.
2) If possible, take a photograph of yourself so that you can also contemplate how you may look to others.
3) Once you have completed these tasks, write a brief description of your experiences and your reflections on them. Describe your own impressions of "yourself as another."

Part 2

As an outcome of having completed Part 1, you will have noticed that your identity (who you are) is very much dependent on the things you attach to yourself and on the social and ritual contexts in which those things are associated with you. You will have noted, in other words, not only the specific ways your ability to negotiate socially is dependent on the everyday contexts within which your identity unfolds, but also that those settings are characterized by familiar symbolic things that identify who you are to yourself and others.

The goal of this second exercise is therefore twofold: (1) to facilitate an active engagement with your reading and thinking about things and places; and (2) to facilitate some concrete understanding of the consequences of specific modes of thought on local action. We want to explore, in other words, the ways symbolic action influences one's sense of belonging to a particular place and to see how modifying symbolic space changes both your identity and the objective meaning of your local environment.

Once you have thought about how meaning is a construct of what Goffman calls the *presentation of self*, you now need to see how the meaning of place can equally be modified and enhanced.

So, in the coming days, try to do the following:

1) Design a symbolic space that is appropriate to the values of your local community (however defined) or to the transformation of those values (i.e., try to create a space that gets others to think about something that really matters locally).
2) Develop that symbolic space so that other people can participate in it (i.e., cultivate that space so that it either invites in specific sorts of people for whom it may matter, or encourages a general public to rethink an everyday assumption).

To devise a symbolic space that has local meaning, it is important that you begin with an analysis of the local social environment through some consideration of the issues that came to light when you altered your identity for a day. Think about the setting in which your identity unfolds and your presentation of self in that setting.

Once you have given some thought to what you learned through your altered identity experience, try to come up with a design for a space that has special symbolic meaning. The process of designing such a space will, in itself, necessarily be controversial and difficult because one of the hardest things one can do is study analytically an environment in which one is at some deep level already emotionally invested; it is also difficult because others may be unwilling to validate your assessment of what constitutes social meaning. Your friends may wholly object to what you are doing.

The reason you were asked to dress differently was to make you in some small way aware of just how much the habits we take for granted are socially constructed, to sense experientially how local and variable are the worlds of meaning we create within a given society or culture, and to sense that these are all negotiable at some level. We need to recognize, in other words, that there are always options out there that are real to us that we have not yet thought of. Knowing this fact at the experiential level is important because stepping out of habits even momentarily alerts us to how powerfully symbols function outside of formally sanctioned sacred spaces. The object with which you cultivated meaning can also help you reorient yourself symbolically.

Being about place, this exercise has another part. You were asked in Exercise 1 to think about not only the meaning of your object, but also about where you kept it and how that influenced your behavior. Now, if your object is something you carry with you, put it in an important place. If you already keep it in an important place, for the time being leave it there. Once you have deposited your object securely, go off and engage in some menial task that takes you away from the object. If possible, find your way into a large building—an office building school, or another nondescript environment, preferably a place without windows. Find a comfortable spot to sit down and close your eyes. With your eyes closed, raise your hand and point in the direction of what you think is the special place where you left your object.

Open your eyes and determine if you got it right. If you did, you are beginning to approach what it is like living as an indigenous person who grows up oriented in a symbolic landscape: you are sensing what it might be like to be a Balinese or an ancient Greek who had a sacred mountain to orient actions toward; you are understanding better what it may have been like to be a medieval European who when disoriented in the forest would look for the local church tower—the house of God—or listen for its bell. You have begun, in other words, to sense how in moments of instability you can take concrete actions to restabilize yourself symbolically. You are beginning to understand how everyday actions can remain unconscious until the need arises to make them more meaningful. You are beginning to see that being the average American who moves houses every 3.5 years may not be all that healthy.

And if you failed at pointing in the correct direction, think about where your object has been placed—the location of your ritual space—as you go through the coming days. Think especially about how knowing where it is can help reorient you when you feel out of sorts. The exercise will eventually teach you why Mt. Kailash, Mecca, and Monument Valley cannot be replaced at any cost—how symbolic awareness makes you more alert to and responsible for your local world; how local values can build inalienable relationships to real places.

Finally, consider if there are ways in which the issues that are the focus of your project might be brought to the attention of a local community or group of individuals. Are there constructive, life-enhancing ways of involving others in the symbolic space you have created? When you have given this project a week or so to unfold, try to assess what you learned from the exercise and how you might convey what you have discovered to others.

CHAPTER 2 | A Sense of Place

Nemo dat quod non habet
(No one gives what he does not have).

—ROMAN LEGAL PHRASE

1. Ordinary Commodity, Uncommon Oddity

I have come to believe that if history were recorded by the vanquished rather than by the victors, it would illuminate the real, rather than the theoretical, means to power; for it is the defeated who know best which of the opposing tactics were irresistible.

—DEREN (1953, 6)

A few years ago, while attending a conference held in the former family home and vineyard of the great French physiologist Claude Bernard, I had a singularly moving experience. On my way to the second-floor seminar room of this remote and tranquil country home, I noticed in the estate's small museum a display case containing two quivers. Approaching the case, I thought it likely, given Bernard's famous interest in curare, that these were ethnographic artifacts, probably of Amazonian origin. Yet I was at great risk of missing that day's meetings when I read that one of the two contained the very curare arrows that had been given to Bernard and that, in turn, had aroused his curiosity. Here, in other words, were the very things—the intellectual property of an Amerindian whom we will *never* know—to which the modern discipline of anesthesiology and its great consequence (namely, the pharmacological amelioration of suffering) are indebted.

51

The year was 1844. The arrows and quiver had been collected from an unidentified Amazonian two years earlier by a man named Goudot. We know nothing of the individual who, by giving them, helped shape the field of anesthesiology. Every patient undergoing open-heart surgery is indebted to him. Indeed, what modern medicine might look like without this discovery is hard to imagine.[1]

But what is also remarkable about this exhibition is its empirical concreteness. Were curare to be discovered today, its molecules would immediately be synthesized and patented (as those of curare eventually were), and the messy and still dangerous arrows discarded. But the quiver and arrows belong here in rural France; for here, both the history of modern medical practice and the abuses of indigenous intellectual property rights remain quite humbly and starkly embodied—right here, in this place, this quiet room of a former country house.

Today, some 170 years later, we are finally asking why the Amazonian who gave us curare and those who shared his knowledge of its use were never even thanked, let alone rewarded or reimbursed. Is simple human greed the reason, an unwillingness to share the profits of such a discovery? If so, are there ways of protecting the disadvantaged from the oppressive strangulation of multinational corporations and the individuals they hire to expropriate indigenous knowledge? If not, why have we neglected to compensate him? Is it because our notions of property are incommensurable with indigenous forms of knowledge? If so, why have his given way to ours? If not, why has he continued to lose out? Is it because we know his dilemma but have no clear way of reciprocating? In such an instance, what can *reimbursement* mean? And how do we reimburse? Does our confusion about how to do this arise from the fact that the process of globalization homogenizes our views of what matters? If so, how can indigenous peoples resist the temptation to comply with these overwhelmingly seductive trends? If not, how may we learn to see what can be morally gained by an appreciation of what is unique about those lifeways, the rituals that give them local meaning, and the places that are in such ways meaningfully changed?

These are major questions of our era—all of which come into focus when we imagine that Amazonian holding out his curare arrows to the waiting hand of one Mr. Goudot. How may the outcome of such gift giving be bettered for the giver? And what can anthropology offer toward its betterment? To answer these last questions, we must first understand what we ourselves are doing when we commodify knowledge as property; even the most basic anthropological assessment will reveal that our universal assumptions about the ownership of knowledge are themselves eclectic and culturally driven.

As Coombe (1998b) and Strathern (1999) both clearly show, facilitating some awareness of how culturally peculiar are our own property practices is *the* fundamental contribution that anthropology can make to any and every discussion of intellectual property rights. And, if one is tempted to think this a rather nonspecific goal, one need only recall just how late today's politicians and environmentalists have been in attending to the issue of indigenous rights—to culture, to heritage, to place. Time after time the colonial records have remained completely silent on the mere existence of indigenous inhabitants within colonial territories, and any examination of the romantically motivated environmental literature will readily show how recent is the inclusion of indigenous peoples into the environmentalist's puritanical, if not openly dehumanizing, view of the landscape.

2. Glass Bead Games

> Capital is a term for assets, whether in the form of money or otherwise, which are used for the purpose of making more money.
>
> —CHERYL PAYER, *Lent and Lost*

Before one can buy and sell knowledge, one must first find some means of quantifying it; in quantifying it, one must first give it a name, establish a provenance, and at least suggest a range of experiences to which it might apply. Failure in any of these endeavors can undermine both a claim to own that knowledge and, in turn, its marketability.

In some indigenous systems of thought, the buying and selling of ideas—even putting them out to bid—is not only a familiar but also morally acceptable activity. More often, however, this is not the case. Increasingly vocal indigenous groups have rejected the concept of intellectual property outright, claiming that it is based on ways of thinking that are unfamiliar and, indeed, immoral.[2] Musing, not long ago, over this problem of incommensurability—of what ideas are and how they may be exchanged—I came across a description of the first encounter between Rudyard Kipling and Mark Twain that seemed perfectly to encapsulate this predicament.

Kipling had journeyed from his new home in Brattleboro, Vermont, to Twain's home in Elmira, New York, to pay a visit to one of his favorite literary heroes. As Stuart Murray points out in his wonderful book on

Kipling's Vermont, Twain later wrote of the encounter with Kipling: "I believe that he knew more than any person I had met before, and I knew that he knew that I knew less than any person he had met before...." Twain told his wife: "Between us we cover all knowledge; he knows all that can be known, and I know the rest."

Like most else of which Twain made humor, there is a dark message here that makes the absurdity of his remarks the more tragic: we all know that there are modes of understanding that are not easily given over to the sort of schoolboy fact-knowing that Twain saw in Kipling's control of knowledge. Is "the rest" that Twain claimed as his own a kind of wisdom that comes of experience, or just the plain ignorance allowed for by his typically ironic turn of phrase? At one level, his comment is just funny. At another, it's an extraordinary insight that carries with it the implicit awareness of so much that cannot be known, in the sense of being spoken of or written about—let alone labeled, classified, or owned.

So what, one may say? If indigenous peoples have ways of knowing that escape the myopic views of hardened capitalists, it is unlikely that those same capitalists would ever be in a position to steal traditional knowledge. Things are, however, not so simple. The fact that a Balinese friend of mine allowed me to photograph a sacred piece of wood (on the grounds that the god would—as it did!—jam my camera if it did not approve of photography) would not keep me or anyone else from seeking patent rights for a product derived from that species of tree were we to explore its medicinal properties. One does not, in other words, have to understand the indigenous view of some plant or animal to profit from its efficacious by-products. In fact, to benefit, one need not at all be aware of the broad levels of symbolic and metaphysical integration that are part of what give that thing ritual meaning in its indigenous context. Nor is it necessary for one to see that those same levels of integration also bind that indigenous person to his or her landscape in ways that make turning the natural world into a commodity both conceptually problematic and morally unacceptable. It is these broader domains of knowing that philosophers refer to when they speak of ontology, embodied knowledge, and moral value.

How do our beliefs about what moves the cosmos influence our daily practices and the cultural artifacts (the knowledge) we create to give presence, and a sense of permanence, to those beliefs? How does understanding what someone is trying to do connect with what that individual believes to hold the world together?

Here, then, we come to anthropology's first, and perhaps its central, contribution to the issue of how indigenous peoples might be honored for what they know, for how ritually they know it, and for how meaningfully they attach that embodied knowledge to a given place. The anthropologist, like the increasingly world-wise indigenous person, is positioned at the threshold that separates what is locally known and what exogenous information must be known for survival. Only here is it possible to establish the degree to which specific indigenous ways of knowing advantage or disadvantage individuals and groups as they attempt to make their way in a monolithically capitalistic world. Here, in other words, is where we must begin if we intend to gain some grasp of why indigenous peoples have not been better positioned to claim what would be, under more favorable circumstances, rightfully theirs.

So, thinking about such mysteries of human difference, I found myself having great sympathy for Twain in his encounter with the young and precocious British author as in the same vein I could not help also feeling sympathy for so many indigenous groups that have never subscribed to the idea that knowledge can be converted into a commodity or at least to that notion in a way that would allow them a modicum of success in today's global markets. And what constitutes success exactly?

This is an enormous problem, and one that is all too frequently left out of discussions of the procuring of intellectual property rights for indigenous peoples. Part of the reason for this lacuna is the top-down perspective of policymakers and even advocates who themselves are immersed in the legitimization of their own organizations. It doesn't take deep reflection to see that it is not only the World Intellectual Property Organization (WIPO) that is caught up in getting those who ignore it to accept its authority: any day at an international meeting at which vested political and economic interests are represented will reveal that the reason the emperor has no clothes is because he has given them to his brother who is attending in the guise of that country's Minister for the Environment.

When an international organization's own credibility hinges on accepting the sometimes bogus claims to sovereignty made by the so-called leaders who have bought into the international status quo, it is we who reify and legitimate those international systems by allowing them to negotiate and legislate morality at such a remove. It is we who read newspapers, watch television, and waste countless hours discussing the private habits of those very politicians who have enslaved themselves to various forms of institutional life that are often at odds with local knowledge. These activities increasingly occupy us, moreover, at the expense of the kind of daily interactions that might otherwise have sensitized us to what is really feasible when we set out to think up the world anew.

Whether or not an indigenous group is properly represented, then, is crucial; but representing at all is complicated by our endorsement of international rules of entitlement that overlook the diverse, sometimes problematic, ways authority is recognized and secured. This being so, how do indigenous peoples come to learn the nuanced, self-legitimizing language that is spoken at international congresses? How might they understand the degree to which those same international groups "are mutually recognizable, produce similar documents, speak a common language" (Strathern 1999:197) and collectively reify their identities as experts? This is why, at the level of selfishness, the neoliberal Left and the neoliberal Right often appear indistinguishable.

While those who attend international conferences may actually be legitimating the transnational institutions they believe to be responsible for undermining indigenous autonomy, their mere presence also, if passively, endorses the process by which the diverse moral worlds of indigenous life are homogenized. Even anthropologists who find themselves defending indigenous rights must, like those who lead delegations and represent their countries in the highest capacities, bow and scrape to their so-called peers in other countries because they need those peers to legitimate what they themselves are doing. As I said to a deeply committed friend in one such setting, the problem with these meetings is that they have become so immunological: one can no longer distinguish the antigens from the antibodies. Clothing, alas, still goes a long way toward inducing certain behavioral responses, which is why a photograph of an indigenous delegation strikes us as so tragic. And there is no reason to think that certain indigenous values about property are any less different from the diversity that gets exaggerated publicly in the courtrooms where indigenous rights are negotiated.

But there are even more complex reasons for suppressing indigenous modes of thinking in intellectual property debate. If *tradition* is not understood monolithically, it becomes very difficult to identify the group one is meant to be defending.[3] The Sierra Club may be unwilling to subsidize Native Americans who have opted for life in a Phoenix plug-in trailer park over their relatives who are willing to remain at home on the candle-lit range.[4] But how, we may ask, might a Native American seeking out the right to maintain ritual property avoid the double-bind in which any choice is a losing one? Stay at home and have one's resources taken, or get a degree at the local university and risk losing one's traditional epithet.

Alas, anthropologists might have been more help here than they have been; it is both disgraceful and disheartening to find us quibbling over how best to assist the less fortunate in procuring their intellectual and cultural rights—especially those who, in calmer times, were the object of a more remote fascination. One almost hesitates to put to print a record of the sad battle that ensued for years between the American-based organization, Cultural Survival, which promoted the development and management of indigenous resources as a way of hopefully promoting a fairer participation in the market economy, and its British-based parent, Survival International, which saw such activities as "at best a money-making gimmick and at worst a harmful idea" (Corry 1993: 2), the effects of which may be precisely the opposite of those intended. Indeed, the very existence of a movement for traditional resource rights (Posey 1996) is a testament to the fact that many indigenous groups now see in the transformation of indigenous property and forms of knowledge into commodities "only the spread of Euro-American forms of property that will legitimate the extractors of resources and make it more not less difficult to promote indigenous claims" (Strathern 1999: 186).

To feed up a laundered notion of indigenous peoples as in themselves harmless and by us harmed,[5] especially while some sponsored groups apply their profits to the purchase of chainsaws, aircraft, and even automatic weapons, might give one pause when reflecting on "our" role as protector of "their" rights.[6] But indigenous peoples who have witnessed their peers being shot by loggers and gauchos can have only a diminished sense of the world's longevity and their participation in it. Apocalyptic images throughout the history of Western art and literature have amply illustrated the human tendency to seek immediate gratification in the face of imminent annihilation. Ronald Reagan, too, believed that the sale of America's natural resources was justified by the coming Armageddon (Vidal 1988); how, then, can we blame indigenous peoples for exacting what they may perceive, in a precarious moment, to be their just rewards? Who are we, anyway, to say what constitutes a just remuneration?

If, however, we are to transcend stereotypical and highly rarified description of indigenous life, how do we avoid attributing to others the same disease of greed that we assume is endemic in global settings? Are others just like us, or are they not? As we know, oppression so often thrives on dehumanizing what we consider different. The practice of using demeaning terms to justify the most appalling forms of oppression is, for example, widely documented (Leach 1964), and even hinting that members of another society might also suffer from their own tyrants—that is, to describe them as we might one another—will do nothing if not erode the novelty that makes possible our fascination in the first place. Even more troubling, ought one instead mount "a worldwide outcry demanding respect" (Corry 1993: 2) for the rights of indigenous groups while knowing full well that seeking distant alignments between do-good organizations and oppressed Fourth World peoples[7] can actually advance their victimization by local power brokers who, once advocates disappear back to the city, punish locals the more severely for having spoken out (Stoll 1995)?

Let us remember that these culprits may well be those same "leaders" who appeared at last week's international meeting claiming that the indigenous problems of the world were sorted out long ago by the vague language of the Biodiversity Convention signed by 126 Heads of State.[8] Here, it is critical to acknowledge that codes of professional behavior that have been independently developed, signed, and publicized[9] have had a very limited impact on the cultural cleansing of indigenous peoples by their economically driven oppressors. If one cannot even get governments to ratify property conventions, imagine what the average gaucho might think were he to read its recommendations during a siesta from tree cutting. In the vicious throes of survival and human greed, he now must contemplate some manner through which he might

> respect, preserve and maintain knowledge, innovations, and practices of indigenous and local communities embodying traditional lifestyles relevant for the conservation and sustainable use of biological diversity and promote their wider application with the approval and involvement of the holders of such knowledge, innovations and practices and encourage their equitable sharing of the benefits arising from the utilization of such knowledge, innovations and practices. (Article 8[j])

Well, yes, this is a start, but common sense tells us that the likelihood of such language having *any* impact on human behavior in the rainforest is, for the moment, exceedingly remote.

Show me a single indigenous group that has fairly benefited by multinational exploitation and that has, in turn, successfully redistributed among its members the rewards of that arrangement, and I will be the first to say that this transcendence of the socio-economic problems that plague the rest of the world might be swiftly remedied by a careful examination of those indigenous institutions that made this equitable transference of assets possible. The problem, in other words, with seducing indigenous groups to transform their natural resources into commodities is that the process itself often so disrupts their lifeways that even they themselves may be caught between the preservation of those lifeways and what is required to succeed in the arenas of international exchange. How, in short, can indigenous peoples both exist in "local communities embodying traditional lifestyles" and in international settings where they must compete with multinationals for the preservation of their intellectual property? Who, in fact, could manage at all under such expectations?

Without painting too depressing a picture here, I need to remind myself of what it was like to be a member of a committee convened to assess a draft of the first ever intellectual property accord between a major corporation (The Body Shop) and an indigenous group (the Kayapó of Brazil). The very language of the document—and indeed its very title—got weaker and weaker with age: at first a contract seemed likely, but a contract is a legal document, and the Kayapó, being then neither a corporation nor a politically autonomous body, were in no position to enter into a binding contract that might be at odds with existing Brazilian policies and that in any case could almost certainly never be policed for them by their national government. To the contrary, where the presence of indigenous peoples on exploitable land provides de facto tenure and entitlement, removal of those individuals by homesteaders is all too often pursued clandestinely (Ellen 2006). Indeed, almost any kind of proposal for international agreement could similarly erode an already tenuous relationship between indigenous groups and their overlords, and those who feel that enough visibility in the media might guarantee the safety of indigenous peoples who demand their rights need only channel-surf now and again to find that yesterday's heartbreaking vignette has been replaced today by an infomercial on food-rendering products or by a new episode of *The Simpsons*.

So, shelf life is a real dilemma facing Fourth World peoples—one, furthermore, that goes broadly unrecognized: first, because we rarely question either the source or the longevity of our own enthusiasm for novelty; second, because a respect for another nation's autonomy (including its right to oppress its own minorities) seems always to remain the sine qua non of international relations.[10] And who were these representatives of The Body Shop anyway to meddle in the affairs of a sovereign country (Coombe 1998a)? So, instead, we were left, for that moment at least,[11] with the word *covenant*—a word of no legal consequence, but one that, so we hoped, might perhaps embarrass other, less considerate corporations into feigning a concern for the rights of indigenous peoples.[12] In the meantime, as we congratulated ourselves for behaving morally, indigenous groups around the globe were being daily eradicated for their unwillingness to accept the world's view of them as helpless and needy. Indeed, those who actively resisted colonialism continued to be the most aggressively humiliated, and those who shunned international congresses were simply ignored.

So what good is anthropology then in promoting the intellectual property rights of indigenous peoples? What do we learn here that is at all encouraging? What we learn, in the first instance, is why it is important to embarrass corporations[13]—why it is immediately necessary to call attention to those silenced indigenous voices by insisting on a covenant, if not a contract. But this is not all; what we also learn through attending to differences of culture is just how important it is now and then to leave behind the bright lights of those international meetings in favor of local indigenous initiatives that are better tuned to some specific moral world—to the ritual spaces and places that resist being transformed into commodities.

And then there are the well-intentioned local advocacy initiatives: so often between that candlelit dwelling and the big university there exists a grass-roots organization—a small community college, for instance—struggling to meet the needs and to better the lives of its indigenous poor. These settings, without doubt, can also be morally and politically complicated, but at least one's involvement at such a level may be adjusted on a daily basis in light of some real sense of what may be feasible. At least one is aware of the meaningfulness or meaninglessness of gestures made by all of those people in expensive suits who yearn to be seen at conferences, in hotels, over long dinners, behind the closed doors that protect them from the kind of real life that they so much fear living. For one thing is quite clear: left to their own devices corporations will always seek to extract the greatest possible profits. So why should they inherently be at all capable of policing themselves either morally or ethically?

Having spent time in not only small colleges but well-known research universities, I hate only to pick on the latter; but their policies are by virtue of their research and funding concerns much better articulated. They are also the ones I happen to know. Take, for example, the following passage from the Harvard Medical School's (1990) "Policy on Conflicts of Interest and Commitment," which begins by claiming that moral scrutiny is essential, and ends by washing its hands in wishful thinking (1):

Public trust in the enterprise of academic medicine and the legitimacy of its powerful role in society require a constant amenability to public scrutiny. Consequently, it is necessary at this time to ensure the continued confidence of the public in the judgment of researchers and clinicians and in the dedication of academic research institutions to the integrity of the scientific

enterprise. The strength of this assurance is based on two assumptions underlying the explicit rules and implicit norms governing faculty behavior at the Harvard Medical School:
* that the vast majority of scientists are honest and conduct their research with the highest standards of integrity; and,

* that for the vast majority of cases, self-regulating structures and processes in science are effective.

Based on these assumptions…cooperation between industry and academic medicine is consistent with the highest traditions of the medical profession and can energize scientific creativity.

Indeed! One need only consider this statement in the context of the medical school's huge indirect cost surcharge for faculty grants (that's a direct charge levied by institutions against grant givers) and the fact that industrial laboratories daily tempt away its researchers to perceive the school's own potential conflict of interest and to imagine just how much suspension of judgment is actually required to sustain this particular cultural myth about the superabundance of human goodwill within a bastion of self-interest. Where so much of what people do depends on the profits secured through ownership of intellectual property, it is no wonder that institutional review boards are so busy. This is in an esteemed setting of presumed integrity—imagine what it must be like in the gold-mining camps of the Amazon basin. So much for Alan Greenspan's odd notion that capital markets are morally self-regulating (Warde 2011).

3. Minding the Gap

Sin is for one man to walk brutally over the life of another and to be quite oblivious of the wounds he has left behind.[14]

—SHUSAKU ENDO, *Silence*

We need not make the topic of modes of thought the exclusive subject of this chapter to realize that we cannot make too much of the topic itself. In light of the complex turf that now constitutes what is and is not heritage (cultural or intellectual property), it is easy to see that an indigenous person is unlikely to negotiate successfully the sale of her rights to her own genes if she cannot manage to succeed in the market for Brazil nuts. For even among those who ought to know better—namely, among bench scientists who make their livelihoods patenting the molecules they have synthesized—what actually may and may not be patented is rarely understood with any precision. This, after all, is why so many tax dollars are spent on the salaries of patent and copyright attorneys and on the government examiners who award these privileges.

In other words, to own something one has to know what the ground rules are for establishing what the word *own* might mean: *Nemo dat quod non habet* ("no one gives what he has not"). While the simple Calvinist reading of this Roman legal phrase translates something like "you can't give what you don't have," the original Latin also makes possible a wonderful play on words: the singular noun *nemo* allows us, as it did Jules Verne in *20,000 Leagues under the Sea*, to personify this "Mr. Nobody" (this Captain Nemo) who loses his identity in attempting to give what is not his or to offer something that is actually nothing.[15] In Latin, in other words, there is deeply embedded in this saying the idea that it is both impossible to get "something for nothing" and wrong to think that one should: "A 'no one' tries to give what he doesn't have"—or, even more damning: "One who has acquired immunity (legally or by deceit) from giving a part of him/herself in what is given, risks losing all means of reciprocating with his/her fellow citizens": "if you don't know how to give part of yourself in what you give, you are nothing, an outlaw ('without the law')."

Though this final interpretation seems far-fetched to modern-day capitalists, it was very much understood in the context of the social obligations of Roman citizens—citizens for whom the *nexum*, the institutionalized exchange relation of two people, was predicated on a fundamental idea: namely, that the process of giving and giving back could not survive if the giver was not somebody willing to stand behind what he or she offered by becoming a literal part of it. Civilization, in other words, could survive much, but not trickery in trade and certainly not the cynical elevation of tricky dealers to culture heroes. Odd, then, that we should find the Late Roman Empire an emblem of society's dissolution, especially since in the absence of social responsibilities the social rights our corporations enjoy would have seemed outrageous to those same classical forbears. Let's face it: the reduction of the Fourth World to a permanent service sector is not going to be reversed by allowing a corporation to move abroad every time citizens ask it to improve its benefits program.

If only it were possible for those very Romans to view us as we glorify Wall Street cheaters who export themselves, their flight capital, and their corporate identities to wherever they may extract the greatest trade advantage. What sad paragons of nothingness our businessmen would appear;

for they have absolved themselves not only of the responsibility of creating goodwill in society at large, but more tellingly, of liability for what their corporations do. In fact, this is the explicit meaning when a company calls itself "Limited." (Ltd.)—a limiting of personal liability for a corporation. In America, such protection for executives had, by 1886, been made official when the Supreme Court ruled (*Santa Clara County v. Southern Pacific Railroad Co.,* 118 U.S. 394 [1886]) that those who ran corporations should be exempted from what the corporation did, and that the business itself should enjoy all of the rights granted to people—which, as we have seen, is why a corporation can own intellectual property whereas an individual cannot if the art is known to more than one person (i.e., is in the public domain). Corporations are, as it were, slaves of their executives who themselves remain largely protected when the drone misbehaves or goes bottom up. The corporation, then, is now a person, while its chief executive officer becomes a nobody.

So how do traditional peoples compete in a game where the deck of cards remains this unfavorably stacked? Well, in short, they don't; ironically, the identification of a corporation as a legal person also means that it has personal rights that indigenous collectivities do not. Corporations are, for instance, permitted "to spend unlimited sums to defeat environmental initiatives, because campaign spending limitations have been ruled to interfere with their right to free speech" (Pope 1996).[16] In 2010 the United States Supreme Court made that even easier by ruling in its Citizens United decision that businesses as people could suffer from oppression of free speech, opening yet another opportunity for making false claims that were clearly not in the public interest. Increasingly, even hedge funds managers argue that losses may be the result of their corporate "persons" being victims of human rights violations.

Because of their individuality, companies can, moreover, possess rights to trade secrets that groups of traditional peoples cannot; because the ideas of the latter are in the public domain whenever those ideas can be shown to be known by more than one person. What this means is that several employees of a company can share knowledge of a patent owned by one company (that is, one legal "person"), whereas an unincorporated group of tribal people do not share the constitutional or other protections of corporate personhood. To put it simply: why protect corporations and not indigenous groups?

The problem is made worse at the level of defining what social responsibilities that corporate person may or may not have; because a corporation, unlike a real person, has individual rights without social duties, a fact that has led it to be described as a person "without a soul" (Perkins 1999).[17] And if one, against all reason, persists in thinking of them as the socially responsible players they claim themselves to be in all of those public radio advertisements, a healthy discussion about the merits of the North America Free Trade Agreement (NAFTA) with any citizen of America's Motor City—Detroit, Michigan—would provide a proper, if not an edifying, reality check. In fact, flight corporations are so good at moving and hiding their money that today a full one-third of the world's monetary wealth remains unaccounted for.

Combine the corporate person with an increasingly flight-driven notion of capital,[18] and one can see that, were it not for the advocacy of certain anthropologists and social activists, it might be time for all indigenous peoples to throw up their hands and surrender. Where market success for indigenous groups rests both on alien definitions of knowledge and on competing against the personhood of a corporation, one can see how the issue of indigenous rights procurement begins to look, as we say, rather academic. And remember: these conditions will continue to prevail regardless of what we do to address the practical matter of how rights might be concretely procured and regulated in the unlikely event that an indigenous person decides against all odds that he or she wishes to pursue them.

4. Body Shop or Chop Shop?

> So out of the ground the Lord God formed every beast of the field and every
> bird of the air, and brought them to the man to see what he would call them;
> and whatever the man called every living creature, that was its name.
>
> —GENESIS 1:19

One of the primary dilemmas faced by indigenous peoples in the procurement of rights to their own heritage—to the ritual objects and places that embody their tangible heritage—is that so many of the precedents for the rights to heritage stem from cultural property, and particularly from cultural return, cases. Here, entitlement is a function of its inalienable connection to a group of people who collectively value it. This issue has been addressed by a number of anthropologically oriented researchers who highlight the disjunction between cultural property (the ownership of which depends on collective knowledge over generations) and intellectual property (the ownership of which depends on showing that what one person knows is new).[19]

Groups' rights to knowledge (except, of course, for our personified corporations) run against the grain of what we mean by invention. In patent law, as we saw in Part 1, the main criteria for awarding patent rights to an individual are that his or her invention be new, that it be useful, and that it be nonobvious. It is, of course, the last of these that is most problematic for indigenous groups, since shared knowledge (except, again, for corporations) is, as we have noted, always obvious to those who share it. Nonobviousness is therefore the trickiest criterion, but essentially it means that the idea would not be obvious to anyone normally skilled in the art in question.

By current understanding to continue our earlier example, the fact that more than one Guyanese native knows that the greenheart nut induces estrus in mammals (i.e., that it is a natural means of birth control) automatically places that knowledge in the public domain and therefore outside the reach of any potential owner: there is no "non-obviousness" to the process of simply suggesting that one eat a greenheart nut for purposes of limiting fertilization. By contrast, of course, the individual who synthesizes a molecule of greenheart so that it may be marketed as a pharmaceutical product can and will succeed in controlling its manufacture and sale, as the process for isolating the compound may be patentable—which is why corporations are so well positioned to profit on the heritage knowledge of others.

Setting aside the enormously complex issue of how one translates remunerations into a local system of value,[20] this is also, of course, why no Amazonian is likely to receive a single penny for any of the successful open-heart surgeries that were the outcome of an ancestor having given his curare arrows to Mr. Goudot. It will do no good to take your native recipe, chants and all, to a court of law—unless, that is, you have enough benefited from advanced training to enable you to synthesize your own molecules, to seek out patents for them, and to defend them vigorously against transgressors.

This last idea—beating capitalism at its own game—is a difficult, though not always an impossible, task. Where the political incorporation of an indigenous people becomes feasible, advantages may, in fact, be collectively realized. Some Native American groups, for instance, have on occasion used their political autonomy to reap significant financial gain in markets excluded to others. Gambling is one example; a concession for harvesting natural resources is another. Though the odds are greatly against indigenous interests, they are, sometimes at least, not insurmountable.

Yet even the most autonomous and powerful of political bodies have difficulty competing with corporations that are not burdened by geographical allegiances. A multinational is just that: "American," say, when it comes to needing military escorts to transport its oil; "Liberian" when it comes to avoiding expenses on the tankers that transport it. One could wonder equally how willing the Liberian army might be to protect those tankers and how the taxes otherwise levied on those tankers might be put to some use in America. The First Gulf War, that is, made much more apparent than precision bombing.

Add to their ability to change national allegiance the fact that multinationals can shift capital with even greater ease, and one has no trouble imagining why indigenous groups repeatedly find themselves at the mercy of corporations. After all, if rich multinationals are able to bring politicians shamelessly to their knees, those corporations should have no difficulty subjugating the indigenous groups to whom those same politicians have so often denied basic human rights.

Against such odds, one favored response of indigenous peoples has been to remain silent about what they know. While making lots of noise can call attention to their predicament, it does little to afford real assistance to those who have been disadvantaged and may, in fact, attract more predators who hear from a distance the cries of the wounded. Though many indigenous groups and their advocates protest unfair trading practices, the grotesque profits made by big business often make the greed of industrial shareholders that much greater.[21] So, simply demanding justice will probably have little or no effect and may actually work adversely. It is unlikely that military flyovers of indigenous lands will be halted because they shake the very bones of the spirits that reside in the clouds. However, an anthropologist can at least draw attention to the dilemma and can do so in a way that is artful enough to show, as Margaret Mead put it, what any person with an ounce of good sense might plainly see. A simple map of Australian aborigine dream strings or a totemic map of sacred sites will do more to show how unamenable are indigenous notions of ownership to modern concepts of property[22] than will any political rally or beautiful photograph. As Benthall points out, "the game is for high stakes, but cool and trained attention to the rules and to ways of changing them is likely to be more effective than moral indignation (1993:3)."

We will get more specific in a moment, but first we must be aware that copyright, in addition to secrecy, is a major means of protecting what we know. The problem with copyright and trademark, to return to a point made earlier but not fully argued, is that they protect not ideas but the way those ideas are made public. How many ethnobotanists know that publishing one's field notes as a book may actually strip the rights of the knowledge described from those whose knowledge they profess to honor? While one may not without acknowledgement copy a document, or without a license a patent or a trademark, what one *tells* in one's writing is placed within the public domain by virtue of its copyright. I can, for instance, talk to you about the greenheart nut without acknowledging its main proponent, Conrad Gorinski, but I may not cite without quotations his manner of describing its use.[23]

And it is because of the potentially disastrous implications of making knowledge public that secrecy remains the time-honored way of protecting ideas—in both modern and traditional societies. The problem, of course, with secrets is that they may be stolen and their rights awarded to the thief. The other problem, especially for traditional peoples, is that secrets more often than not die with their owners. Attempts to remedy this problem have involved the construction of different types of *commons* within which information can be both regulated and shared, including for instance "natural resource commons, social commons, species commons, and intellectual and cultural commons" (Srinivas 2012: 408). There are also a number of open-source biopharmaceutical initiatives that "allow conditional access to members and opt for the joint management of knowledge assets" (ibid.: 412). On the one hand, such initiatives represent fair practices of information sharing; on the other, more valuable secrets are generally less collectively shared and more rigorously policed—which is why, as noted earlier, covens of shamans may so effectively be compared with modern-day patent-pooling cartels.

Here, the advantages for those who have access to resources and to knowledge are obvious: new patentable discoveries may, through license or through deceit, be built on another's recent invention without actually having to understand or untie that earlier knowledge.[24] Furthermore, the same invention may be remade in a different way that allows for the procurement of a separate, new patent. This process—called *reverse engineering*—is what has made so many electronics manufacturers wealthy. Just take it apart and rebuild it in a different way. Let us not, therefore, forget the real consequences of simply having or not having access to recent knowledge, even to recent knowledge that resides within the public domain.

In England, for example, a company named Oxford Analytica has done very well for itself by regularly convening academic experts from the university to offer among other services up-to-date assessments and feasibility studies for corporations planning business ventures in the most favorable locations around the globe. This is, of course, business as usual for companies that need to know just how cheaply they are likely to build and operate a soft drinks plant in West Africa; but not being a player at this level means that Third World countries—despite their rich base of knowledge—become effectively reduced to an enslaved workforce for the First World. While some countries have laws that are meant to prohibit the importation of goods made by slaves, we have few ways of knowing when goods that appear to be the outcome of fair labor practices are actually slave produced and then laundered through front companies. The problem, moreover, will only escalate when buying into these front companies has boosted already rich economies and made the rich so much richer. Though Oxford Analytica will now gladly sell its knowledge to developing countries as well, the political reality persists: all policymakers who applaud NAFTA and the General Agreement on Tariffs and Trade (GATT) for creating financial health in the West should at some point in their political career be required to abandon the air-conditioned hotel and escorted fact-finding tour in favor of an honest day in the field. For I know of no anthropologist who would dare argue that a laborer in America or Europe ought to be capable of succeeding in markets where the ground rules in human dignity are so negotiable.

One must remember here that market success in patentable knowledge functions no differently. Indeed, in some ways it is more viciously contested, since courts may overrule a person's right to his or her own patent if the owner fails to exploit that idea in a timely way. So, not only has "free trade" now created more false-fronted shops than a Colorado mining town, but also if you decide not to mine your own claim in a timely manner someone else may be rewarded handsomely for extracting your very ideas from under you. Even assuming, in other words, that indigenous peoples learned all the ropes of international trade and patent law,[25] it would be unlikely in the extreme that they might recruit the necessary resources to halt the reverse engineering of a legitimately awarded patent.

And then there are the flagrant violators. We promote the myth that laws are enforceable across national boundaries,[26] but how many visitors to Taiwan built marvelous libraries out of bootlegged books? While trademark and copyright owners spend millions pursuing counterfeiters, what free trader, after all, will aggressively pursue such violators when windfall profits accrue to merchants who turn a blind eye to the origin of counterfeit goods? Is it any wonder that international trade meetings lead so often to protests, anger, and hostility? Open competition, we all know, never rewards reticence, except of course if you are dead sure that you own something that others cannot obtain. This, after all, is why Sotheby's does so well on the Upper East Side and in Mayfair.

5. Uneasy Resistance

Taking means in nearly every case being taken.

—FANON (1966: 182, referring to the oppressed)

While the odds against indigenous peoples may have been more or less stacked since the days when Europeans first thought it profitable to trade with them (and fully cemented by the Age of Discovery), the record of indigenous resistance is equally as old, even if we tend to ignore it (Scott 2009).

When Caesar entered the Lowlands for the second time in 53 BC to try bringing down the resistant tribes, he was not prepared to fail. Like American forces in Vietnam, the Roman militias, despite their ingenuity and sheer size, were unprepared for indigenous forms of resistance. Caesar demanded allegiance, yet what happened? His plan was as it had been elsewhere: bring tribal leaders together; impress them with the fact that they will cooperate; offer them a piece of the power if they do so; even offer to eliminate their local enemies. But in Gaul this did not happen: when Caesar invited local leaders to a summit, some representatives just didn't come.[27]

Every time indigenous people knowingly ignore the rhetoric of domination, they may indeed be exercising their freedom, for to liberate themselves from the oppressor they must ignore rather than resist. This is what social theorists mean by the term *hegemony*. And understanding hegemony as it works on the ground may be one of anthropology's greatest contributions to the intellectual property debate. It doesn't take much to sense when one is being coerced (Scott 1985), though many nonetheless fail to appreciate the effects of their own coercion. This is a big claim; but it has its merits in the realm of truth. As we have seen, nostalgia about a romanticized native past repeatedly provides no real solution for indigenous groups because it requires an ossification of native identity that by definition disempowers indigenous peoples from adapting to ever changing circumstances.

Similarly, the righteous protests mentioned earlier often can produce effects opposite to those intended, because focusing on unfair trade rather than empty indignation allows us to see the difference between simple oppression and hegemony. As Gramsci stated emphatically, hegemony thrives on *unequal engagement*, a dynamic "combination of force and consent variously balancing one another,...an active and practical involvement of the hegemonized groups, quite unlike the static, totalizing and passive subordination implied by the dominant ideology concept" (Forgacs 1988: 423–24).

Because political commentators and journalists have widely taken up the word hegemony as a fanciful replacement for the word *domination*, even social theorists now fail to understand how hegemony functions. Few realize that in exercising this failure they too are actively participating in Gramsci's hegemonizing process, since equating the terms, without attributing any volition to the oppressed, actually cements the very idea that oppression is inevitable, that the strong outlive the weak, and that the oppressed will always be subject to oppression.

Those who participate in contests or structures where status terms are recognized by both oppressor and oppressed are not challenging hegemony; they are acknowledging it. Members of the Hells Angels Motorcycle Club who affiliate with a congress of gang members—including a president, a sergeant at arms, and various elected representatives—may be undermining what white-collar politicians in Washington, London, and Brussels are up to, but the action also functions to acknowledge, if mockingly, the power that these ruling classes possess.

To ignore the call of a reciprocity that is, by nature, self-stigmatizing is to be a nobody in the eyes of those who stigmatize. Not recognizing authority, that is, promotes the most dangerous form of liminality; for what the genuine outsider stands for is a breach of the sort of heroic and egotistical values that are otherwise everywhere to be seen in society at large. This is precisely why some indigenous peoples have called for a refusal to accept the terms laid out by Western governments (no matter how favorable), by the corporations that sponsor those governments (no matter how lucrative the rewards),[28] and even by the advocates who seek intellectual property protection for indigenous peoples (no matter how loudly those advocates claim to own the moral high ground).

Native Americans are probably best positioned (given their legal semi-autonomy relative, say, to Amazonian tribals[29]) to attempt this line of free thinking. Indeed, since pursuing legal rights to knowledge one already owns "forces indigenous people to play the dominant society's game" (Greaves 1994: 6), some indigenous spokespersons call for an outright refusal to accept the economically driven terms of legal ownership that have been invented by capitalists for their own benefit. However, even at its best—that is, where freedom can mean the ecstatic pleasure of creative liberation—the tactic of denying the authority of an oppressor is very dangerous, particularly in an age of cultural homogenization in which the ability to respect real difference of viewpoint becomes about as rare as the desire of most Americans to learn a foreign language. For those displaying the extreme arrogance of thinking they can live without capitalism, the most ruthless forms of punishment are often exacted.[30]

The more political autonomy a group has, the more it not only can claim its own corporate rights, but the more it is empowered to ignore the status demands of social and political hegemony. When the Dalai Lama refuses to comply with an interview request from television personality Diane Sawyer, he does much more than make sure he still meets a group of anonymous people in Ohio to whom he had already committed himself that day. By ignoring requests from important people in favor of talking with commoners he both transcends the bleak realities of the everyday and offers some hope to the disadvantaged that they too may find transcendence. What we see in such behavior is, therefore, complex: on one hand an expression that transcends the otherwise inevitable oppression of a punishing world; on the other a creative realization of the joy and liberation that successful transcendence gives rise to.

This is why the freedom to create is actually more basic than a bill of rights and why creativity can never itself be fully measured by any single set of intellectual property terms. This is, moreover, also why many anthropologists feel that the first step to securing intellectual property rights for indigenous peoples is to secure their political autonomy. The problem is that Brazil is no more likely to offer such freedom to the Kayapó than is the United States to return to the State of Vermont its former status as an independent commonwealth.

6. An Honest Day's Fieldwork

A woman generous with both her friendship and her ideas, she left the latter lying around like pencils, she said, in the hope they would be stolen.

—WILLIAM MITCHELL (on the ideas of Margaret Mead)

Twenty-five years ago I set out to learn if certain medicinal plants that had been brought to my attention during research on other matters had either been previously studied or might be studied to good humanitarian effect. In writing this book, I therefore had an excuse to dig through old and fading files; my interest in so doing stemmed from a distinct impression I still carry around that I had failed in my effort to call attention to the potential medical value of what had been openly offered to me by "indigenous" friends. At the time, I naively believed that creating new and useful knowledge could have only a beneficial outcome.

Today I am very thankful for not having set down that road. However, reading over a typically disinterested response from a pharmaceutical company, I at least know now why it is a good idea not to throw away every old letter. Though ethnobotany is itself a now matured discipline—indeed, as ancient as the specialization of healing itself—one cannot make too much of just how recent is the surge of interest in the subject and in its related intellectual property concerns. The overinflated expectation that Merck Sharpe & Dohme's molecular prospecting agreement with Costa Rica's National Institute of Biodiversity (InBio) will result in a true canvassing of the economic potential of that country's botanical resources (Sittenfeld and Gamez 1993) must be placed against the background of what I was then told: namely, that there was a time back in the 1950s (i.e., before computer-based molecule building and testing) when companies had a go at canvassing the rainforest, but the results had been very disappointing.

Part of the reason for this disappointment, of course, was the fact that research then was no more ethnographically informed than were most of the World Bank's development projects in the Third World during the same era. The hideous concept of cultural capital (that was meant to quantify and to corral local ways of behaving—that is, indigenous habits—into economically productive forms of behavior) had yet to be thought up, and corporations were just as out of touch then with indigenous knowledge as they are today. Indeed, given the homogenizing effects of technology and of the English language on all of the earth's inhabitants, it is probably a safe bet to say that the potential outcomes of what might be learned are actually far less today than they were in 1950. And despite all of the treaties and international conferences, it is probably also fair to say that even the most enthusiastic capitalists who now want to patent other peoples' genes so as to preserve (read: own) them[31] will not equal what was learned by one man named Goudot who took that curious interest in the knowledge of a single Amazonian native.

Against the idea of cultural capital, anthropology has offered the notion of indigenous knowledge for development (IKD). While this concept will still raise the ire of those who believe that such intervening measures seek to make indigenous peoples into unsuccessful capitalists, at least the idea has enough of the ear of those who work in international development to indicate some need to understand the extraordinary diversity of indigenous ways of thinking (e.g., Sillitoe 1998). To date, the idea has been favorably received by a number of government and nongovernment organizations,[32] and it suggests at least that anthropology is being recognized as a potential mechanism for avoiding future disasters of insensitivity.

This is not just a boastful call for recognizing the importance of anthropology in intellectual property debate or, more importantly, for developing human respect and genuine cooperation among diverse peoples. Nor is it simply an attack on the culturally unadventuresome and methodologically sterile predispositions of bench science.[33] Corporations will continue to sign contracts with other corporations or governments rather than create bonds with unincorporated indigenes for reasons that we have already considered; if they are at all concerned with their images, those same corporations will refuse (at least publicly) to deal with vigilante ethnobotanists who wrongly see indigenous knowledge as the best thing since the California Gold Rush.

Politically correct investors who think that they are supporting native peoples merely by buying stock in corporations that attempt to work with indigenous groups (e.g., The Body Shop, Ben and Jerry's Ice Cream, or the late Shaman Pharmaceuticals) should ask themselves whether or not their money wouldn't be better spent on a college-level course in political economy; for the shareholders of any corporation are equally capable of attacking their executive officers for failing to behave in financially responsible (read: economically aggressive) ways.[34] What is more important still is the fact that even the most altruistic relationship between a corporation founded by a venture capitalist (e.g., Shaman Pharmaceuticals) and an indigenous group will, as it becomes increasingly profitable, create havoc. Shaman's early losses made it, at first, an ideal focus for the watered-down sympathies of humanitarian capitalists, but the problem looks more complex when the United States Department of Agriculture (USDA) finally gets around to allowing a darling company its monopolies on plant- or animal-derived drugs that may (like Taxol) have a real impact on cancer or (like Salagen) reduce the negative side effects of cancer therapy. The staggering financial outcomes will, in other words, eventually be apparent without attending to how far they are from the conceptual framework of those natives who gladly sold their oil concessions for a bag of trade beads.

Even Shaman's 20% local contribution to indigenous peoples was apparently figured on their prospecting budget (Burton 1994) rather than on future royalties. And to whom would they give the profits anyway? Certainly not directly to the shaman who offered them the indigenous knowledge. He is, as this same favorable article politely acknowledges (ibid.) feared for his deadly powers by his own neighbors, and his case is anything but anomalous.[35]

While Shaman commendably tried before going bankrupt to build schools, purify water, and promote social welfare, such outcomes, we must remember, will be only as good as that, or any other, corporation's commitment to a local moral world whose very human rights are not otherwise, or only minimally, protected. Indeed, access to a working knowledge of what is locally feasible not only may allow for more realism among award-winning environmentalists who wear their badges so proudly down those stuffy hotel corridors of their international meetings, but also may facilitate a genuine capacity on the part of indigenous peoples to respond most appropriately to an inevitably changing world.

Though what anthropologists do may so often be imperfect, our discipline—as practiced by us or by indigenous people themselves—may, in the end, have the only monopoly on the translation of cultural categories of thought. And though translating categories may strike us as an abstract and academic predilection, its real implications are everywhere to be seen when we get down to the basic business of not walking over one another. Humble though working at ground level may appear to high-flying policymakers, it is here where even those policymakers will contribute most.[36] As Posey once said, the anthropological contribution toward indigenous control of indigenous knowledge will only be realized "when anthropologists become researchers for and consultants to indigenous peoples and traditional communities" (in Sillitoe 1998).

Anthropology's contribution, then, to the future of what intellectual property might mean—both for indigenous peoples and transnationals—is critical: first, in demonstrating what sorts of initiatives may actually be feasible; second, in using a knowledge of what is feasible to become a good advocate for indigenous peoples who have less access to global resources; and third, in showing how advocacy must be situated in a dynamic notion of culture that allows for indigenous groups to be as much or as little like others as they themselves want to be—a dynamic notion whereby we wish more for them than that they either be what we are or what we are not.

What indigenous peoples need to protect their intellectual property is a better understanding of how to establish reciprocal relations with those who have benefited from them—whether those beneficiaries are corporations that have synthesized indigenous therapies or anthropologists who have gained professionally by illuminating indigenous forms of knowledge. Since there is no way to reciprocate without reciprocating, a willingness to "marry in" is essential. There needs, in other words, to be some form of moral investment.

The new schools built on today's charity to promote the development of indigenous groups will only be as successful as the quality of the intellectual property courses taught within them and as durable as the commitment, intelligence, and compassion of those who teach those courses. This, then, is the main role of anthropology—to show how essential it is to live and love in places not only where the lights are not very bright, but even in places where such lights, at least as of yet, do not exist.

PRACTICUM 2 | Valuing Indigenous Property

THE FOLLOWING LIST OF suggestions and questions are meant to assist readers in becoming directly involved in the issues raised in Part 2.

Readers are invited to review this brief list and to think about how they might involve themselves in rethinking what property could mean when a moral investment makes it inalienable. In particular, consider the complex issues that arise when symbolic property is commodified, and how symbolic investments can disadvantage those unwilling to commodify financially what they value.

1) How does turning a place from a deeply symbolic thing into a commodity make it easier for us to leave that space and the system of local knowledge that is cultivated around it?
2) Are there ways the increasing tendency to pick up and leave one environment for another can be reduced?
3) Are there organizations that define themselves as protectors of symbolically meaningful places?
4) Are these organizations positioned to learn from indigenous forms of cultivating local symbolic meaning?
5) What are those organizations' strategies for defending environments from being treated as commodities?
6) Are those organizations positioned to contribute to the real issues faced not only by indigenous groups but also by anyone who desires to create local forms of meaning that are not readily translated into fluid capital assets?

7) Are there ways organizational strategies might be improved
   or redirected?
8) How could you contribute to that improvement through
   the forms of engagement you discovered through Exercises
   1 and 2?

EXERCISE 3 | Giving and Receiving

OUR THIRD EXERCISE IN this small book is designed to introduce you to the effects that valuing symbolic objects in symbolic spaces (what is often pejoratively labeled *animistic* behavior) can have on systems of exchange. Exercise 1 asked you to animate an object of your choice. In Exercise 2 you focused on attaching special meaning to your immediate environment and examined how this activity concretely influenced your daily behavior—how actions can be made more symbolic, even creatively ritualized. The present exercise invites you to experience how animated objects can convey important aspects of yourself at the social and ritual levels through systems of symbolic exchange.

To achieve this goal, permit me by way of suggestion to summarize a system of exchange in which the symbolic merit of objects is actually elevated by forms of reciprocity that are locally and individually negotiated. Though other kinds of symbolic exchange might be described, I like talking about the Melanesian system of exchange called kula. I like it not only for the simplicity and elegance of the system, but also for its careful description in the ethnographic literature over a long period of time and by men and women both. That is, we can study it, if we wish, from the standpoint of gender symbolism as well as from the standpoint of well described theories of exchange. At the risk of oversimplifying, I want to review briefly a few of its essential features.

In Melanesia, off the coast of Papua New Guinea, lie the Trobriand Islands. There one finds a well-known form of symbolic exchange called kula. In kula highly prized objects, specifically arm shells and necklaces, are circulated in opposing directions over many years and across great distances of ocean in a grand circular system whose size and scope transcend the individual lives of the participants on which its fragile successes so much depend. Every object given is part of the giver. Every participant takes a necklace from one exchange partner and gives one to the next partner along the line. That same participant takes an arm shell bracelet from the opposite direction and passes the one he has to his previous partner. One takes one object from the right and gives it to the left while taking a different object from the left and giving it to the right. Two circles of exchange occur: one clockwise, one counterclockwise.

In this way, one always gives a type of object that is different from the type one receives. Objects increase in merit as stories and related amulets are attached to them. Other sorts of commercial exchanges accompany this symbolic activity; but the fundamental point is that whatever object one currently has becomes the focus of understanding important life events that transpire while possessing that thing, and that (because of its presence) rich legends accrue to the object over time as it circulates. The *kula* object, in other words, not only carries the fame of the original owner, but of all of the owners who possessed it during its years of circulation. Kula is a system of trading and enhancing inalienable value; but unlike an object enriched for commercial trade by naming its provenance (as, for instance, a thing once owned by a famous person), the kula object eventually returns to its original owner as a symbolic testament to that person's place in the world.

The idea of kula is to create as large a trading ring as possible: too small and one's fame will not be carried abroad; too large and one may risk the ring breaking entirely. The system, in other words, must be constantly monitored so that an object of merit produces trust. One has to trade a thing of symbolic value, or one cannot produce the need for a return exchange. One also must know one's limits or lose out entirely through failing to induce the appropriate commitment from one's exchange partners.

Though participants may hope to succeed in cultivating a system of exchange that spans hundreds of miles of open ocean, taking at times years to come full circle, the minimal trading group is a group of three: the owner, a trade partner in the clockwise direction, and a second partner in the counterclockwise direction. By this means a trader can take one sort of object from the first partner and pass it to the second, while taking a different kind of object from the second partner and passing it to the first. In kula one symbolically mediates, that is, the flow of objects in two directions, always having an obligation to one partner that is fulfilled by what one receives and enhances from another exchange.

Because each object is a part of the giver, every trade results in the passing of something, the meaning of which always increases. Objects are kept and stories are attached to events that take place while the current owner possesses that object. Events, in turn, are also attributed to the power generated locally by the object's presence.

Kula demands an acute awareness of local symbolic space and one's place within it. This being so, success in kula is considered the greatest form of human relation. By contrast, holding oneself away from such exchanges leaves one alienated, or, as Trobrianders say, "hard on the kula." The kula world is filled with animation, filled with knowing one's environment through giving oneself to it, filled with seeing oneself in another. In kula there are no free gifts; for every gift carries with it an implicit catalyst for a return gift. For every prestation, there is a counterprestation.

Over the years, I have tried in many classroom settings to create systems of kula with objects animated by students. Some do not take the exercise seriously, finding it difficult to offer a cherished personal object or an animated heirloom to another person. But others become completely committed to experimental kula. When they do, the results are extraordinary; for kula not only alerts participants to what has been lost through exchanges of commodities, but also creates in itself new relationships that often last for years. Unsurprisingly, this kind of exchange is actually accessible even to the most hardened capitalist; for in succeeding participants learn how contracts are kept, while in failing they see what is lost when symbolic property is commodified.

So, the idea behind this third exercise is to try to establish some system of symbolic reciprocity whereby others can be brought into your symbolically energized world through dynamic exchange relationships. This exercise can be demanding, but it also can be extremely rewarding and creative. Though how your exchanges are structured and cultivated is entirely up to you, the following steps will help you get started:

1) Try to imagine what conditions might be necessary to create enough trust in others to allow you to offer even temporarily something personally important in exchange for something you believe to be deeply important to your exchange partner or partners. What could you say about the object you are giving that would increase the chances of the person with whom you hope to exchange treating your prized object with respect and deference? How can you convince that person you are giving a genuine part of your being when you hand over a thing that is so much a cornerstone of your identity? How can that importance be expressed so as to generate trust and commitment in both parties?

2) In consultation with your partner or partners, design a system of symbolic exchange that meets the same criteria as the kula exchange system. Specifically, design a system whereby you are a giver to one person in the system and a receiver from another. Then see if you can now be a receiver from the person to whom you gave and a giver to the person from whom you received. What can you do to encourage your partners to take the exchange to a new creative level—that is, to generate enough interest in your relationship so that the outcome for your object is actually an enhancement of its creative, symbolic value? How can that object's strength be shared and nourished? How can that enhancement in turn produce not only interdependency but also a state of general well-being? How can that state of well-being be brought to reflect favorably not only on recipients but also on original owners who will, if the system is sustained, eventually receive back their enhanced objects?

3) Between now and the end of the exercise, keep a careful journal of your system and the objects you exchange.

How have daily events been influenced by the presence of your exchanged objects? How has your personal object's meaning been transformed by its having been part of a complex symbolic exchange? Has the growth in an object's value altered the conditions under which you are willing to exchange it? What, if any, difficulties arose in making your system work? What were some anticipated and unanticipated outcomes? How have your exchanges influenced your relations with other members of your exchange network?

4) Try to determine what is gained or lost in a free market economy where things are exchanged as commodities. Why, for instance, do meetings of the World Trade Organization so often lead to protests by angry citizens? Is it right that fully one-third of the world's financial resources remain hidden? Is it right that 60% of American corporations pay no taxes? Is it appropriate that corporations have the ability not only to avoid taxes but also to move their goods and services freely across national borders? What would Mauss and others who studied kula exchange have said about the North America Free Trade Agreement and the General Agreement on Tariffs and Trade—agreements that turn once producing economies into service economies or leave them wholly impoverished?

5) Are there ways you feel you might influence either the organizations that oversee trade or those that lobby against unfair trading practices by encouraging others to reenergize objects with symbolic meaning? Are there new ways to think about how the physical world might be more meaningfully understood, ways that conform better to today's new and emerging needs?

All Greeks were peasants. They did not deserve such
wonderful works of antiquity.

—SIR DAVID WILSON, Director, The British Museum

1. "Tradition Is the Enemy of Progress"[1]

In her study of disputed cultural property, Jeanette Greenfield (1989: 47) refers
to the Elgin Marbles as the *cause célèbre of* cultural return cases—in part
because it remains probably the most long-standing and most publicized
cultural property dispute, but also because it is emblematic of the effects of
colonial imperialism on designated cultural treasures. I do not intend in this
chapter to expose the degree of prejudice that led Lord Elgin and others to
feel that the moral order dictated "that Britain should keep the Elgin Marbles
because Britain is the 'true heir of Pericles' democracy'" (Moustakas
1989: 1179). Nor is it my goal to critique the ludicrous argument that could
lead one to think that a plate by Donatello is rightly an inalienable piece of
British heritage because it was discovered in an English country house; that a
painting by Bosch is Spanish because the Prado got it via the Hapsburgs; or
that a Stubbs portrait belongs in America because a Mellon paid for it.

I want to talk about evolving cultural identity not because I intend to focus on any one of these fascinating, if bizarre, examples of rhetorical chicanery, but because I wish to make a particular kind of argument about the relationships among cultural property, capital accumulation, the dissolution of symbolic networks, and the moral reciprocities that are central to ritual. This argument is not Marxian; it is rather about what happens when the dissolving of symbolic networks allows for the random accumulation of hidden, uncommitted, financial wealth.

What I will not do, therefore, is take up directly the issue of repatriation of objects (though in most cases clearly such objects should be repatriated); nor will I focus on how cultural assets have been appropriated or stolen (this being the focus of Part 2). What I will do is examine an area that has been ignored in this highly politicized and contested domain: the increasingly frequent situation in which a deconsecrated object is considered a commodity by both buyer and seller.

It is hard enough dealing with, say, Balinese traditional art, where the only distinction between a piece of national heritage and local airport art may be the consecration of the former; but it is harder still when we try dealing with a once significant piece that has become, through deconsecration, less meaningful or simply meaningless. I have seen, for instance, ancient Indonesian ritual vessels gladly sold to tourists who were destined to use them as ashtrays; and I will never forget arriving at the home of a Balinese carver of important ritual masks, only to find him busily carving "African sculpture" for export. If Donatello can be construed as an inalienable part of British heritage, why can't a Balinese adopt Africa?

In the highly polarized domains of the market's contested good and evil, one can easily fail to account for the following facts: that many once inalienable objects have, for whatever reason, lost that inalienable status in their culture of origin; that when certain objects are perceived only by some as inalienable the relevance of such objects will be contested from within their culture of origin; and that the identities of many of these objects, including those brought out both before and after their indigenous status was lost, will be revitalized in the interest of constructing new notions of culture or new political identities.[2] It is under such conditions that objects become the focus of cultural contestation and also under which we become, as it were, immunologically paralyzed by a particular rhetorical strategy about *tradition*. What conservative humanist (Highwater 1985: 235) can, after all, stand up and say that the Greeks are not entitled to Macedonian artifacts because Alexander the Great was not "Greek"?[3] What worth, after all, has international law if we can openly contest the static construction of a Greece, an India, or an America?

In what follows, what I hope to show, therefore, is not so much that the peculiarities of contemporary repatriation strategies are part of a pattern in which the definition of culture is disputed—internally, externally, and over time. What I will try to show is something perhaps more important: that the loss of cultural wealth is frequently accompanied by social disintegration. To return to my original theme, I will argue that marbles (not only Elgin ones) have, in some cases, been lost coextensively with, or even in advance of, having them taken.[4]

It is in considering also these deconsecrating processes that understanding the destiny of cultural property becomes significantly more complex and more problematic than our cultural swan songs (our hero epics about saving others) will permit. Do our own salvation narratives hold such sway over what we can say or even what we allow ourselves to think? Certainly the romantic marginalization of traditional peoples as both needy and anachronistic signals the degree to which themes of epic salvation have led to a self-imposed moratorium on how we can view cultural property. Indeed, some traditional peoples have been fully appropriated by a messianic environmental movement that once, by definition, excluded them. Meanwhile, the rest who fail to conform to the environmentalists' ossified stereotypes of loss and salvation simply have no voice. As one Hopi Tribal Council member put it: "I don't have to dress dirty and live in a hovel to prove that I'm traditional to white people" (Conason 1986: 26). His anger was sparked by the decision of an environmental group to provide his tribe with legal and financial assistance, but only to "real" Indians.[5]

In what follows, I will argue that the existence of vast areas of neglected discourse (about how issues of cultural property may be constructed) points directly to the rhetorical power of particular, culturally valued heroic narratives of loss and slavation—epic stories that themselves discount and, ultimately, eliminate cultural difference along with other forms of experience.

2. Booty, or Losing One's Marbles

There are simply too many cases in which one may examine the appropriation of otherness in the cultural construction of selfhood to warrant any kind of inventory. So forgive me if I set aside the many would-be Hapsburgs who appropriate cultural artifacts as statements of political superiority or the modern-day tyrants who collect the diverse forms of religious art from within their own countries as a means of claiming political legitimacy or the politicians for whom the repatriation of ancient works of art amounts to a legitimization of their own political authority.

What I want to do is to go right to a case that offers both internal and external contestation over an object of great symbolic power. Then, at the end of the chapter, I will conclude with a more general consideration of how the redefining of inalienable wealth makes possible the appropriation and neutralization of indigenous forms of power, of soul loss—truly losing one's marbles.

The best case I know in which the internal and external contestations of an object's meaning are played out simultaneously is one that for reasons unknown to me has not been taken up widely, but one that (fortunately) is carefully examined by Holm and Reid (1975) in their study, *Indian Art of the Northwest Coast*. I want to spend some time with this case and focus on their analysis because we so easily assume that those cultures that request repatriation are themselves static, stable, and uncontested. In this example we see something probably far closer to the realities of how cultural identities are negotiated and of how objects figure in such negotiations. We also see, by contrast, what happens when people fail to engage in their own kula exchange.

The story begins sometime in the late nineteenth century when a small group of individuals, led by Lieutenant George Thornton Emmons (1852–1945) and the Victoria physician Charles F. Newcombe, developed a deep interest in the nonprofit collecting of Northwest Coast artifacts as a means of preserving Indian culture—almost all of which, at that time, had little or no financial value. They practiced a kind of applied ethnography, collecting with the purpose of preserving artifacts—a philanthropic collecting. Emmons, in particular, sent thousands of artifacts to museums and became so close to the Tlingit that he spoke of them in the first-person plural and was accepted by them as "the son of a noble warrior" (Holm and Reid 1975: 15). As a highly positioned military man (he became an admiral), Emmons pleaded the Indian case to Teddy Roosevelt and is probably the person we can most credit with the remarkable fact that so many known Northwest Coast artifacts are in public hands or recently repatriated to tribal museums (ibid.: 16).

But it was actually a Tlingit and a museum collector who were at the center of the dispute I am about to discuss. The Tlingit was Louis Shotridge (1886–1937), (ironically) the grandson of a tribal nobleman (Shartrich) who had been Emmons's close friend and confidant. At the age of nineteen, Shotridge met Dr. George Gordon, the director of the University Museum in Philadelphia. The two began a working relationship: Shotridge joined the museum staff, assisted Gordon as a "museum Indian" in lectures to schoolchildren, and became the guest, friend, and eventual companion of such important figures in the field as Franz Boas, Frank Speck, and Edward Sapir. Though Shotridge's father was a chief, Shotridge was an alcoholic, as were many members of his extended family. "Home was mud, boredom, alcohol. Gordon offered escape....Shotrdige stereotypically proved a great success, popular with school children, a favorite of the press, the hunting companion of Theodore Roosevelt and John Wanamaker" (Holm and Reid 1975: 18). Shotridge, in fact, presents us with a much truer image of the liminality of those who step forward as negotiators of traditional cultures in cosmopolitan settings. Here, permit me to venture from my redaction of Holm and Reid and quote at length their version of the story (ibid.: 20–22):

> Unlike Emmons, [Shotridge] didn't limit offers to pieces no longer in use or no longer valued. Offers he made in Klukwan [his ancestral home and center of Tlingit art] greatly exceeded the sums he paid elsewhere for comparable pieces, yet were generally rejected. In the end, he tried to steal the Rain Screen and houseposts from the Whale House in Klukwan.
>
> These particular pieces, by general consensus, were the Tlingit's greatest surviving treasures. Shotridge had promised them to Gordon as early as 1906, laying claim to them on the grounds his father had been Master of the Whale House. But Tlingit descent is matrilineal. Shotridge had no claim. He didn't even have the right to enter the Whale House, except by invitation.
>
> First he offered $3500. There probably wasn't $100 cash in all Klukwan at that time. He spoke eloquently, at great length, in the Whale House. He said that Gordon was an honorable man, that he would protect the treasures, that they belonged to the world [which, of course, is precisely the argument used by advocates for the British Museum's keeping the Elgin marbles] and would forever reflect the glory of the Whale House. The answer was an unequivocal no.
>
> Finally, with the Museum's knowledge, he laid plans to steal them while the men were away fishing. "We plan to take this collection," he wrote to Gordon, "regardless of all the objections of the community," and Gordon replied, "I am glad you have found a way to overcome the serious difficulties in obtaining full possession." But a "gun went off," narrowly missing him. This traditional Tlingit custom, midway between execution and assassination, was no mere warning. Shotridge sponsored a feast to reestablish peace.

The Depression worsened and the Museum let him go. He received no pension, merely a letter of regret. He was left without means or support in a hostile community. His bank was in difficulty and he couldn't withdraw his savings. He couldn't collect money he had lent others. His food bill had been turned over to a collection agency. Another child was due. He mailed twelve pieces of beadwork to the Museum, suggesting the staff might want to buy them if the Museum didn't. They averaged less than $3.00 each. Only one was purchased. Another was lost.

Finally, he got a job as inspector in the Salmon Canneries, actually a river guard. Nothing better illustrates his status than this despised job. But he had buried one wife. His second wife was ill. He had five children. He was ill. The last known photograph of him shows him beside a small, torn tent pitched in snow. He holds a blackened coffee-pot over a wood fire....

The circumstances of his death are still discussed. At Klukwan, some say he was killed for taking treasures. At Sitka, some say he was killed for ordering a fisherman off the river. The official report states that he 'fell from scaffolding,' breaking his neck. But there was no scaffolding where his body was found. He lay beside a little cabin he had built. Even if his death was an accident, that doesn't explain why he lay unattended, for days, until a teacher took him to a hospital....But, however he died, he died an "outlaw," unprotected by community codes.

Though it is easy to discount Shotridge as one who had "gone over," we must consider the destitute plight of Tlingit in his day. Had he not offered greater sums to his fellow tribesmen? How could he not, even if wrongly, see himself as helping his culture? And had he, indeed, not made an important contribution to the preservation of Tlingit heritage? Moreover, Shotridge was a careful ethnographer who not only collected for museums but also painstakingly recorded every cultural detail (ibid.: 23):

He found that the old speeches, associated with major pieces, were still remembered in all their detail and eloquence; proposals in council to commission a work of art; speeches made in reply; payments made for a work; speeches made when it was worn or displayed; the capture of a piece by enemies; their treatment of it; ransoming the work; etc. etc. He recorded, as well, detailed accounts of the mythic creatures depicted in these works, and detailed myths about the works themselves. Always with attention to detail!...Art, like so much else in Tlingit life, was often used for power. It was even used as a weapon. Shotridge's efforts to acquire pieces still in use were interpreted as a bid for power and fought by the Tlingit at every turn.

Here, in particular, we must face the reality of an indigenous moral code that even the most experienced of cultural relativists would find impossible. The image we are left with is of a man stuck between two worlds; indeed, even his attempt to take the Whale House screen and posts can be interpreted in indigenous terms. He simply lost his bid for power (ibid.):

> I know of no other record, in all the literature of anthropology that carries the reader so far into alien modes of thought associated with art. Reading these lengthy reports, one soon realizes that the physical object was only part of a complex pattern, and at times could become almost irrelevant. Consider three minor incidents relating to the Whale House screen and posts: At a time when there was hunger in Klukwan, the owners rejected $3500, but then left the screen exposed outside, where it weathered badly. More recently, I stopped two roughhousing children from damaging this screen during a feast in the Whale House. No one else seemed concerned, though shortly afterwards they rejected an offer of $750,000 and ordered the dealer who made it to leave. One member of the Whale House, speaking in council, urged that the screen and post be sold: "What is it we Chilkat respect? Power and money. We hire artists. A Tsimshian made the Rain Screen for us. We bought it for prestige and power. We should sell it for the same reasons.

Though one would be mistaken to assume that all objects of inalienable wealth are thus negotiated from within, it is clearly a grave error to assume that most are not, or that those who step forward to negotiate the liminal boundaries between "them" and "us" (say, anthropologists and their informants) are always able to mediate with any success the moral confusion that results. Indeed, if anything, one must *increase* one's attentiveness regarding any form of ethnographic validation that centers on the authoritative claims of informants who are consciously involved in negotiating and redefining the boundaries of their culture. How many anthropologists, furthermore, find that they have been accepted by the people they study but have been provided with an indigenous categorical status that is decidedly anomalous or liminal? How many ethnographers finally find a best informant in someone living on the edges of a society? Liminality has, in other words, a long history, and one that does not bode well for an honest appraisal of the subject at hand.

It is, to put it simply, all too easy for us—in our plight to preserve tribal cultures or to legitimate our own ethnographic authority—to downplay the extent to which an object's inalienability can be contested from within.

It is also far too easy, when epic tragedies are played out in the repatriation courts, to forget the cultural worthlessness of deconsecrated things—things that may well have been bought and sold as alienable artifacts long ago. Is it not our very own commodified world that both imparts a kind of static fiscal status to an object and encourages us to consider the things of others as always being of deeper value?

And where does the restoration process stop? Do we in the end take down Bernini's famous baldachin in St. Peter's Basilica because it was made of the melted roof of the Pantheon? How, finally, do we distinguish the revitalization of traditional power that gets played out in the international courts from the interplay of traditional and external forms that may have led to the expatriation of an object in the first place?

To address this final question we must consider more closely the estate of those who, for one reason or another, have decided that a once inalienable object is now alienable—where spiritual property becomes a commodity.

3. Paradigms Glossed

By the time an indigenous group is willing to market an inalienable relationship or what for them is god-given, one can more or less assume that tradition—at least as it is popularly understood—has been significantly challenged, if not transformed, undermined, vanished. In its place can be found the destitute in search of some cultural haven, the upwardly mobile in search of a more cosmopolitan life, or the enlightened traditional peoples (the neotraditionals) in search of a rhetorical strategy that will most empower them.[6] The first, the destitute, bear new labels to certify their displacement; now they are environmental refugees or simply homeless—the growing hordes of migrant street dwellers provide the paradigm case. The second, those already transformed, become nontraditional, acculturated, voiceless. The third, the neotraditionals, are betwixt and between: often led by their own honorable advocates and sometimes by their own harlequins, such people are enough enlightened about cosmopolitan life to know that it is not for them or, if it is, that its role must be negotiated fully. And because this role requires negotiation, often it is the least traditional people (or most culturally adventuresome) who step forward to represent tradition—individuals liminal enough to have feet in several doors, worldly enough to have learned the hard way how to survive, homegrown anthropologists of sorts.

Eventually, each of these groups unwittingly participates in an extreme transformation—if not the atrophying and silencing—of tradition. Because change is a challenge that some but not all rise to, it is important to focus on why these individuals, in fact, *must* be liminal if they are to realize that what is self-evident on the indigenous level is nonobvious to outsiders and vice versa.[7] Such leaders may be seen everywhere today, and their morality runs the range from saint to charlatan.[8] In some instances, the two are autoimmune, virtually indistinguishable, since survival itself depends on enterprise and enterprise is a function of cleverness. Indeed, the very rapidity of social change has thrust traditional peoples everywhere into a highly liminal world where the awareness of change may be life's single stable feature—where those who step forward to negotiate change must, in fact, distinguish themselves from traditional leaders (whose ways may be blamed as much as honored by them).

The voice of tradition, in other words, may or may not be the voice our morally self-important and politically correct ears actually want to hear.[9] Once articulated, moreover, the voice may be not a traditional one (which by most definitions is not enlightened about modernity and is not culturally relativistic) but a flexible adaptation (which recognizes enough of the cosmopolitan world's conditions of success to be engaged in a dynamic rhetorical engagement).

This is not the moment to discuss in depth the extent to which certain indigenous forms of thinking are, as it were, traditionally adaptive. As the Balinese, for instance, are known to claim, modernity itself is neither good nor bad for tradition. It is how one uses modernity's creations (technological or otherwise) that matters. At the same time, it is worth noting that some indigenous values may conflate stasis and adaptation to such a degree that liminality becomes a major condition of as well as a threat to traditional forms of life—where the resilience of culture is measured not in its static features but in its ability to adapt, and where even apparently radical change may at some level be considered traditional. In such cases, a group may be very much predisposed to endorsing possessive attitudes about both intellectual and cultural property and about what we (and now they) call *art*. A group may also, moreover, be quite willing to articulate, and capable of successfully articulating, that predisposition in surprising ways. My second example, therefore, is chosen deliberately as something of a tonic to Rousseau.

Throughout Christian history, missionaries—whose job it has often been to translate the West into local terms—have been alarmed at the disastrous consequences of their inability to perceive the adaptive powers of tradition, particularly with respect to the ways in which religious categories might themselves be commodified as cultural property. One famous example of such misunderstanding may be evidenced in the so-called "cargo cults" of Melanesia, in which Christianity has been so often embraced because of the belief that God would reward the locals as he had missionaries (i.e., with clean new clothes, plenty of food, and power equipment ["because of Ham's folly, natives could make only outrigger canoes as against steamships, and build houses only out of bush materials as against the galvanized iron, sawn timber, and nails used by Europeans" (Lawrence 1964: 76, f.1)]). Cargo cults are especially useful in discussing cultural property and "art": first, because their leaders are always individuals who have at least some experience of the "outside" (i.e., they are people who might have the ability to grasp something of the economic realities of the cosmopolitan world);[10] second, because the traditional cosmologies in question were and still are sometimes more openly based on commodifying affective relations than we ourselves are when we "cost out" the social value of "cultural capital";[11] and third, because in such situations objects of power (cultural property) and objects of knowledge (intellectual property) can sometimes become indistinguishable.

All anthropologists have at least some familiarity with these systems, but a typical revisioning of Genesis from New Guinea provides the gist quite nicely (ibid.):

In the beginning, God—or Anut, as he was called by the missionaries when they spoke the vernacular languages of the Madang area—created Heaven and earth. On the earth, he brought into being all flora and fauna, and eventually made Adam and Eve. He gave them control over everything on earth and laid out Paradise (the Garden of Eden) for them to live in. He completed their happiness by creating and giving them cargo: tinned meat, steel tools, rice in bags, tobacco in tins, and matches, but not cotton clothing [i.e., they were naked]. For a time they were content but eventually offended God by having sexual intercourse. God in his anger threw them out of Paradise to wander in the bush. He took the cargo away from them and decreed that they should spend the rest of their days existing on the barest necessities. . . .

This situation continued until the time of Noah, who was a 'good' man, obeyed God, and brought up his sons to do likewise. Other human beings were still sunk in 'depravity' so that God decided to destroy them in the Great Flood. Only Noah and his family were to be saved. God showed Noah how to build the Ark—which was a European steamer like those seen in Madang Harbour—and fitted him out with a peaked cap, white shirt, shorts and stockings, and shoes. Into the Ark Noah brought his family—his wife, his sons, and their wives—and a pair of all living animals. Then God sent rain. The waters rose and covered the earth, and everyone else was drowned. When the Flood subsided, Noah and his family went ashore. God instructed them to repopulate the earth and gave them back the cargo as a pledge of his renewed goodwill toward mankind.

Everything would have been satisfactory again had Noah's three sons all obeyed God as he had done. Shem and Japheth continued to respect God and Noah, and so continued to receive supplies of cargo. In due course, they became the ancestors of the white race, which profited by their good sense. But Ham was stupid: he witnessed his father's nakedness. God was again very angry. He took the cargo away from Ham and sent him to New Guinea, where he became the ancestor of the natives, who were forced to make do with inferior local material culture.

What is clearly intriguing here is not so much the fact that indigenous animistic beliefs gave rise to a system of inalienable objects with mystical properties, but that an indigenous system of commodities so accurately paralleled a Calvinism in which ownership of property became proof of God's just reward—that is, where *good* and *goods* became synonymous. Indeed, these cults enough mimic mainstream national and cosmopolitan concerns that they frequently evolve from the periphery of society to its center (Worsley 1968: ix–lxix).

Understanding others, as this case shows, often involves less the problem of appreciating exotic attitudes than of distinguishing between what is actually ours and theirs—where Melanesian concepts of property and European concepts of capital become so similar that the grafting of one onto the other happens without any awareness of the ways the two systems differ.[12] All that is needed is a cult leader (a liminal mediator between the indigenous and the cosmopolitan views of cultural property), who, as it happens, has spent enough time in Sydney Harbour to provide a rational interpretation of international property inequalities. The term *cargo*, in fact, provides a very good tonic for the misperceptions of cultural tourism (Lawrence 1964: 77–78):

In the new cosmos, God was said to live in Heaven, which was believed by some to be on earth as part of Sydney itself and by others, who had listened more carefully to the missionaries, to be above Sydney in the clouds. In the latter case, however, it was thought that Heaven and Sydney were connected by a ladder. The spirits of the dead—the ancestors of both Europeans and natives—lived with God in Heaven. God was continually making cargo, although, according to some, he was helped by the ancestors, to whom he had taught the secret. According to others, however, the ancestors did not make cargo. They merely enjoyed the amenities of Heaven, for which the people yearned so vehemently on earth: European houses with tables, chairs, beds, and other furniture; meals of tinned meat, rice, and other European delicacies, which were served ready cooked by angels; and whiskey, beer, and other alcoholic liquors freely provided for all. There was no shortage of cargo in Heaven: there were stores everywhere, at which personal supplies could be replenished whenever they were running low....

In return for the luxuries of Heaven, the ancestors were expected to perform one special service. When God had prepared sufficient supplies of cargo, they had to carry them to the wharves of Sydney—either to that part of the city inhabited by human beings or down the ladder from Heaven—and load them onto ships that would take them to New Guinea.

If this sounds like a parody of the American Way, the results were equally capitalistic—namely, the wasting and wholesale destruction of local property now taken to be inferior. But parody and irony can also be telling, as David Hecht and Maliqalim Simone point out in their book on African governance. Quoting an unnamed African priest (1994:119–20):

America is a spiritual place....And it is becoming more so. That is why the U.S. is a throwaway culture...not materialistic like Europe. American cars and homes may look lavish, but they rarely last long and Americans are happy to just throw them away. The enormous expanses of wasteland, deserts, junk heaps, and contaminated dump sites in the United States are a testament to how little Americans care about their material world. How their real desires are for things more ethereal and less tangible.[13]

In the Melanesian case, however, the irony was lost: the old was summarily ushered out to make way for the new. Crops were abandoned and pigs slaughtered (ibid.: 94), since modern life not only confirms tradition (i.e., illustrates the meaningfulness of cargo) but also proves that we got, through our own original sin, the wrong end of things: "The local deities always try to trick us into performing the old rituals again in their honor. But what they gave us was only rubbish—taro, yams, and all that stuff. If we yielded to temptation, God would not send us the real cargo—steel tools, tinned meat, and rice" (ibid.: 79–80). Indeed, these Melanesians were completely attuned to the concept of both cultural and intellectual property. To facilitate the arrival of cargo, certain traditions did survive; in particular an indigenous property rule by which "any group making use of ritual to which it had no inherited or purchased rights was regarded as having committed theft" (ibid.: 96). Lest we forget the capacity of some traditions to commodify, it is also worth noting that, in many Melanesian settings, names, songs, and other forms of nonmaterial and intellectual property could be bought, sold, and in all other respects owned. So much for the exclusive sins of our storerooms and museums.

4. Frequent Fliers

Having thus sketched out a system of thought that is, as it were, overly attuned to the commodification of both intellectual and objective property, one must remember that other systems of object relations are so alien to commodifiable categories that they remain only marginally translatable. These I have discussed elsewhere (Napier 1986, 1992). In them, knowledge that comes from the gods entails some attention to cosmology when that knowledge is put to use. Sacrifice is the common form of exchange (no animal in Greece was eaten without it)—where exchange with the spirit world is less often a matter of heated bartering than it is of organized reciprocity; for gods do not look favorably on those who undo them. Reciprocity, in turn, invokes inalienability—that is, the idea that the thing given (as Mauss well knew) carried with it part of the giver (Weiner 1985, 1992)—which, in brief, is to say that unless you can assess how to commodify an ancestral heirloom that has been lost in a flood you will probably have a very hard time determining how the property rights of indigenous people can be valued.

The challenge, then, is this: unless one is willing to entertain the idea that certain forms of traditional property cannot be commodified and to embrace the modes of thought that provide meaning in such worlds, one will never be able to envision any scenario in which both tradition and traditional property rights are protected, simply because the workings of the cosmopolitan world—or rather the bonding process of traditional and cosmopolitan—affects traditional peoples so adversely. The rest, again, is just platitudes and rhetoric accompanied by not a little bit of self-proclaimed goodwill.

Calvinists, despite their love of money, have a very low threshold for contagious magic and, to be blunt, make poor animists (Napier 1992) because a commodity is a fixed, dead thing. As we saw in Part 1, we (ironically) use the term *fetish* pejoratively while at the same time romanticizing the tribal's connection to the land, their artifacts, or their works of art (ibid.). Yet engaging in the sort of mental gymnastics required in situations where an absence of separation between person and thing helps animate an object will, no doubt, be at the center of the greatest challenges to preserving the property of many tribal groups. This challenge makes some unusual demands on us; I cannot describe them all here, but some can be initially sensed through the exercises offered in this book. How, for instance, do we protect property if concepts of alienable wealth do not already proliferate? Can anyone, to begin with, protect something that is not, as it were, owned by an identifiable person or social group? Suffice it to say, in the least, that (because inalienable wealth carries a bit of the owner in the object) healthy bacteria offer the metaphor we adopt when things go right; viruses work better when things don't.

But because the owner—animal, vegetable, divine—is embodied (i.e., is somewhere in there), many non-Cartesian peoples often have trouble excising what we would call morality from the marketplace. A commodity is an object successfully removed from certain affective bonds, and some-times even a completely amoral thing. This is to say that, though "monetization is not a reliable index of the atrophy of the 'moral economy' " (Parry and Bloch 1989: 8), a commodity's crucial exchangeability, its separability from one person to the next, is definitely increased by its ability to shed the appearance of being an inalienable part of someone. Unlike the commodity baron who can steal at work and lead a Bible school on Sundays, many peoples inexperienced in the ways of capitalism are unwilling or unable to commodify their environments to the degree that objects are entirely avulsed from the moral order. The more you see yourself in the thing exchanged, the more you worry on Sunday about where those things have gone and about what role they may be playing in the lives of others. It's a fairly basic idea, which we have now explored at some length.

What is more complex, however, is imagining how objects that are so highly charged actually function ritually. Because these objects carry with them a certain moral weight, they may harbor either that good bacterium or the nasty virus. Moreover, because such objects may have their own powers, they do not lend themselves to a world of commodities in which hopefully moral people interact with objects that are inert and commodifiable (i.e., capable of being valued and fairly exchanged). The kind of legal ethics that works on exchanges from the outside, so to speak, can have little effect on the holder of indigenous intellectual property who perceives that property as possessing an ambivalent power brought into balance through symbolic exchange. Here, property becomes—tangibly—a part of a person.

The international community that does not see itself taking a literal part of the local person with the object taken cannot see when it has ruined a meaningful thing; it also is in no position to see when it is supporting a liminal negotiator who has used, as Shotridge was accused of using, his traditional status to sell wholesale the local moral order. International business assumes that self-interest can be disguised in a cloak of goodwill;[14] in so doing, it exonerates itself of any responsibility for the local ways it now presumes to transcend. Negotiators today invent new nongovernmental organizations as soon as funds appear to rebuild local capacity. It's now an old story, but one that cries out for new kinds of involvement across cultures.

In short, we have no problem in fitting a Rousseau-like innocent picker of nuts and berries into our swan's song about the demise of traditional peoples, but we haven't the foggiest idea of how to address their cosmologies or how to deal with the more complex realities that accompany tragic inequality. If that representative of "otherness" is "a good man," we may lament in our paean the death of some vague mystery that is beyond our grasp. But what if he gets caught between two different kinds of moral order? The point is important: the swan's song has room only for certain versions of the foreign; meanwhile, I'm afraid the Shotridges of the world will die miserably, painfully, and very much alone while their advocates step forward to accept yet more humanitarian prizes.

 | Responding to Global Forces, or Kula International

IN THIS THIRD PRACTICUM you have the opportunity to use your imagination to ask some (hopefully) serious questions about the nature of exchange and the relationship between objects of symbolic or artistic merit and the world of commodities in which everything must have its price. As we now can see, the whole idea of a commodity demands that the values of specific things be universally and uniformly measurable. Stock markets measure daily commodity fluctuations in value, but one share of a company's stock must, by definition, possess the same value as all of the other shares of the same denomination.

Yet, if you are a diamond merchant, you might argue that so much of the value of what you do is socially negotiated, which is why, of course, we have competitive pricing. If value, in other words, is always context dependent (as, say, in systems of barter), the idea of capital is put seriously at risk because capital stability is predicated in any modern economy on the idea that one dollar or Euro is the same as the next. Karl Marx, of course, thought that the social separation of modes of production was the evil that caused capital excess (and he was at that level quite right). But Marx, like most other exchange thinkers of our time, did not believe that an obsession with an object was necessarily a good thing; neither did he accept the notion that such an obsession could be healthy. Our major anticapitalists, in other words, have not always disliked capitalism for the same (or, as Marcel Mauss would argue, the right) reasons.

By contrast, the cultivation of symbolic meaning encourages us to accept Mauss's view that there is no such thing as a free gift. Mauss believed that the more we invest ourselves personally, psychologically, and morally in what we give to others, the more what is returned will enhance both our public and private interactions. Establishing a moral economy guaranteed for Mauss that exchange partners would abide by the forms of reciprocity that are the basis of binding social contracts.

Ironically, over the past decade economists, civic planners, and social theorists have recognized the devastating outcome of the free flow of capital and are now debating how to evaluate concepts of community and communal exchanges—how, that is, to quantify levels of social interaction. Now they've suddenly discovered anthropology (i.e., the study of small-scale local social behaviors). However, rather than asking how value may be ascertained through subtly constructed social interaction, they assume that successful, existing social interaction ought to be measurable and quantifiable.

To achieve their goal of measuring empathy and goodwill, furthermore, they have introduced concepts like social and cultural capital. These managerial notions have gradually gained ascendancy in development circles. However, to an anthropologist of Maussian persuasion, such attempts to quantify the feelings that bind people socially often just look like impoverished efforts to recapture behavior that is not economic or political or consumerist at all, and to present those noncapitalist forms of interacting as if they possessed measurable economic variables. They worship economic models even when economic predictions fail.

By now, it should be abundantly obvious to us that, if nothing else, the entire notion of capital in the modern world is based on an increasing depletion of the kinds of relationships that personalize exchanges by using objects of private value to create social bonds between otherwise autonomous people. Successful social exchanges, that is, traditionally thrived on precisely their local variability and the need, therefore, for each of us to take seriously each and every form of local exchange in which we are engaged. Bartering at the local market is a perfect example: the price paid is never fixed, and the final negotiation is dependent on reading social signals, states of individual comportment, and immediate resource needs.

Free exchanges (and by extension global free trade exchanges) are, on the other hand, very different, since their successes are based on the ability of corporations and individuals to take capital anywhere at any time, and on the assumption that the value of local exchanges are the outcome of universal measures such as stock indexes and rates of exchange. The ability to extract one's investment is what we mean when we call that investment fluid, and the most successful capitalists are those who can keep more capital more fluid than their neighbor next door; there's no second price, as we say, to be bartered when you've filled your car with gas and have to pay the bill.

Because of its uniformity of value, critics of capitalism, then, often argue that capital exchanges are not simply the inevitable outcome of modern transnational circumstance, but are devaluations of local forms of reciprocity and social engagement. This third practicum, then, invites you to tackle this issue head-on by asking you to take a stand on the impoverished moral value of capital. Here are some ways of actively engaging the subject:

1) Identify which areas of professional activity (e.g., policy, exchange law, migration studies, property allocation) are in your view most likely to reshape the almost complete elimination of local forms of reciprocity and social responsibility in the current global economy. Why has kula so openly given way to what we now politely call outsourcing?

2) Determine which political, social, or business organizations and policies are most responsible for this trend, and begin to ask some serious questions. Is a service economy also an enslaved economy? Can governments survive when so much of the world's assets remain hidden? Are there concrete steps by which local moral commitments can be enhanced and relied upon? In other words, don't just blame bankers, or governments, or internet financial practices. Try feeling more confident about how a future might be conceived, and don't let harsh realities defeat your willingness to do something beyond simply protest against changes already made.

3) Determine which organizations are best positioned to redress the increased global absence of reciprocal social contract making. Find them and name them.
4) Develop a strategy for calling attention to the social impact of capital outsourcing. Go back to your thoughts about kula exchange and ask yourself if there are concrete ways you might influence the near absence of corporate social responsibility.
5) If you have good answers to this last question, you have now transcended the utility of this book. So get to work. The world needs you!

PART IV | Realizing Ritual

EXERCISE 4 | Changing Paradigms

THE FINAL EXERCISE ASKS you to imagine the reformulation of what ritual activity could mean within the framework of a reanimated environment. The first three exercises invited you to animate an object, to create a symbolic context for that object, and to consider the terms on which you might reciprocally exchange things that cannot exist as commodities.

By now you can readily imagine how the common distinction between ritual space and daily practice can be dissolved: there can be no distinction between the so-called sacred and the profane once mechanisms exist for transforming pedestrian life into spiritual practice. In this exercise, therefore, we will explore a mechanism by which the symbolic and the real, the spiritual and the physical, become one and the same.

Though initially such practices seem entirely exotic—being widely evidenced in polytheistic settings (e.g., in Tantric Hinduism; see especially Doniger 2009)—it may be of some comfort to modern secular readers that they are at least not wholly foreign to Western thought. Historically, many Christian spiritual exercises, for instance, were designed specifically to acknowledge the fact that symbolic and, as it were, real spaces could be one and the same. And many well-considered arguments about the need for religious investment in material things were based on just such a blurring of the lines between the sacred and the profane (for one such example, see Napier 1992, Chapter 4).

To engage this exercise, then, we begin by imagining ourselves a citizen of ancient Greece or of contemporary Bali. Either
will do, for in both cases symbolic life was often understood in
real terms. Gods and ancestors inhabited a central high place
(Olympus for the Greeks, Mt. Agung for the Balinese).

But since we cannot interview an ancient Greek about symbolic space and we can interview a Balinese priest or priestess,
we will focus on Balinese cosmology. You are free, that is, to get
on a plane tomorrow and visit a Balinese priest and question
him or her about why, say, temples or houses are oriented the
way they are: in Bali it is common practice (though by no means
a universal practice) to orient symbolic property in symbolic
ways. Temples always have a guest seat—*padmasana* ("lotus
seat") for a visiting god. No matter where you go around the
island this seat will be at the place in the temple closest to Mt.
Agung—the place where the arriving god or goddess first meets
the temple shrine when they travel from their mountain abode
to a specific temple to participate in a ritual event.

Houses, similarly, are best oriented so that bedrooms have
beds in which one's more sacred head is directed while sleeping toward the mountain while one's dirtier feet are pointed
toward the sea in which demons and other forms of profana-
tion abound. The Balinese even have names for these orien-
tations. "Toward the mountain" is *kadja*; "toward the sea" is
kelod. Balinese may not always be aware of these directions, but
they seek to embody them as much as possible because knowing them allows for daily behavioral adjustments when things
become unstable—for major events such as births and deaths
and for minor ones such as feeling ill or simply out of sorts.

Now, to this mountain and sea axis we add two other dimensions: high and low (for more and less spiritual endeavors);
and left and right (for good and bad, pure and polluted, white
and black magic). Here again, these axes function in sacred
hundred-year rituals (Eka Dasa Rudra) that are meant to reorient
the universe, but they also function in everyday practice: clean-
ing oneself after defecating is done with the left hand; offering
gifts to others more commonly with the right.

For the Balinese, that is, there exists a three-dimensional set
of tools for reorienting life in moments of major and minor
instability and uncertainty. This system of orientation also has a

ritual dimension: every 210 days (each Balinese year) a temple has a birthday at which the three worlds (of spirits and ancestors on high, of humans in the middle world, and of demons below) are brought together for a ritual balancing. Each village, moreover, has a temple not only for itself (*pura desa*) and for its deceased (*pura dalem*), but also one of origin called the *pura puseh* (the temple of the navel) from which the farther one wanders the more dangerously one get disoriented, possibly snapping the umbilicus if one wanders aimlessly.

And that is not all. The system has an additional cosmic dimension: because the Balinese are reincarnated into the same family lineage, there are explanatory models that assist individuals in staying to local tasks rather than imagining other worlds. If you know that you are coming back to the same place in your next life and returning as your own descendent, your goal shifts from thinking of other worlds to focusing on making this one a better place to live—hence the common tourist's sense that the Balinese are very artistically inclined people who attend in extraordinary ways to the maintenance of their local conditions of living. All of these orienting structures work together to assist individuals in making sense of their place in the world, even if those structures do not always adjust immediately to the presence of unexpected global conditions—like the new accumulations of non-biodegradable garbage amongst tropical peoples for whom nature once did its decomposing quite well.

So this exercise is a simple one. Given what has just been described, imagine yourself living in such a cosmically oriented world. Construct a set of similar points of orientation and cosmic beliefs in your local space. Ask yourself if, under such conditions, it is possible to move elsewhere. Ask how you might respond as a Balinese person to, say, a natural disaster (e.g., the 1963 eruption of Mt. Aqung) or to human disaster (e.g., the invasion of the colonial Dutch in 1906) or to a recent tragedy (e.g., the Bali nightclub bombing of Paddy's Pub in October 2002). And if you were trying to fix a broken relationship, what would you do? If you wanted to circumambulate your ancestral mountain in honor of the gods and ancestors, which way would you walk? Is there an embodied reason for proceeding clockwise or counterclockwise? Finally, what would you do to make

the world a better place when it comes undone? If you were
to meditate on the place you would most like to be right now,
what would it take to make that desired place be right here?

This is, of course, a personal exercise, as I imagine most who
read this book will not live in such an integrated landscape. But
perhaps now is the time to record your own thoughts about
what these exercises may or may not mean to you—even perhaps to consider writing your own book on environmental
behavior. For what we have engaged in is but one of an infinite number of ways of imaging ritual space. It has been pre-
scriptive and provocative, though I hope not too much so; for
each language system that has ever existed, there are unique
ways objects are understood and unique forms of behavior that
accompany those modes of thinking. Some are closer and more
comfortable to us; others are more demanding and exotic.

In this book we have simply tried to inquire about one such
different system of creating meaning and to ask more directly
why animism matters.

CHAPTER 4 | Why Animism Matters

Everyone who has seen visions while light-headed in fever,
everyone who has ever dreamt a dream, has seen the phantoms of
objects as well as of persons.

—E. B. TYLOR, *Primitive Culture* (1913 [1871], 1)

IN 1871, SIR EDWARD BURNETT TYLOR published *Primitive Culture*, at the time a radical book for arguing that animism represented a form of religious practice in which direct evidence of sensory experience got translated into rules, norms, and prohibitions about the body and its local moral world. Tylor's evolutionary view had animism constituting a minimal definition of religion in which the belief that the soul traveled in sleep was evidence for religion's spiritual universality.

That the body was, as Marilyn Strathern (1988) would later have it, partible—that is, divisible by and through experiencing the self as a part of one's behavioral world—raised developmental dilemmas for those who first engaged in studying it intellectually. Following Tylor's lead, many sociologists and anthropologists took up the question of how culturally driven notions of embodiment might create unique forms of environmental behavior. From Mauss's (1923) landmark study of gift exchange through Stoller's (1997) examination of the senses in anthropology—understanding in embodied terms how one sees oneself as a part of one's environment gradually became a central theme in the anthropologies of perception, knowledge, and morality. Throughout its entire history, in fact, anthropology has consistently focused on the effects of cosmology on notions of the body—and specifically on the permeability of the human body image and body image boundary. Because of this consistent focus, anthropologists have often found themselves at odds with those who argue that all humans experience their worlds similarly. Indeed, animism was considered, not only in Tylor's time but still today, by many as an indicator of underdeveloped (or, as it were, "primitive") inclinations. In Tylor's terms, religion evolved from less to more abstract thinking—from multiple spiritual forces to singular, omniscient ones. Just as in psychoanalysis, the baser forms of development (what Freud defined as regressive behaviors) involved a looser body image boundary, a problem of self-knowledge, and a sense of not knowing that required transcendence for advancement and growth. That is also why those who "modernize" canonically indigenous religions so often wish to redefine them in monotheistic terms.

But Tylor's views on animism remain, I would argue, as radical in our age as they were in his. In Chapter 11 of *Primitive Culture*, Tylor (1913 [1871]) lays out how animism—as a base belief that one's local environment is moved by extranormal (i.e., "spiritual") forces—constitutes a minimal definition of religion. This definition is predicated on the notion that a soul (or another spiritual entity) can be capable of an existence independent of that physical body one perceives of as self, and that such an entity (here Tylor followed Auguste Comte) constituted not only humanity's primary mental state but also a condition of "pure fetishism, constantly characterized by the free and direct exercise of our primitive tendency to conceive all external bodies soever, natural or artificial, as animated by a life essentially analogous to our own, with mere differences in intensity" (1913 [1871], 1: 477–78). Though Tylor was later greatly criticized for his evolutionary perspective (where animism evolved into polydaemonism, polytheism, and monotheism) his basic argument had great merit: the notion of the human soul was derived from the need to explain the real experience of dreaming, and ritual activity (most dramatically sacrifice) derived from the twin beliefs that the soul could exist outside of the body and that it could function as a free medium consorting in the space between the living and the dead.

Animism, according to Tylor, depended on an immediate contagious connection between humans and their physical environments as well as on the idea that the soul could be released through sleep, trance, and other liminal psychic states (e.g., hallucinations). In other words, unlike our culturally prejudiced (Judeo-Christian, Cartesian, salvationist) versions of personhood, animism was highly empirical. To wit (following Mariner, in Tylor 1931 [1871], 1: 480]):

The Fiji people can show you a sort of natural well, or deep hole in the ground, at one of their islands, across the bottom of which runs a stream of water, in which you may clearly perceive the souls of men and women, beasts and plants, of stocks and stones, canoes and houses, and of all the broken utensils of this frail world, swimming, or rather tumbling along one over the other pell-mell into the regions of immortality.

For Tylor, it is as if the Cartesian artifice of a solipsistic, indulgent individualism subverts the elegance and intellectual beauty of existential life. Animism allows experiential reality to be faced head-on—perhaps even in a way that today is accessible only to the so-called psychotic soul, as R. D. Laing had it. Viewed this way, animism requires a deep reshaping of psychology and philosophy in a manner reminiscent of the phenomenology of Husserl (1931). In Husserl's initial attempts at hermeneutic transcendence, a basic empiricism is galvanized by a desire to get back to the things themselves. Husserl would not have taken kindly to what anthropologists today call *lived experience*; he was not, like so much of contemporary anthropology, interested in how a perceived attention to high thoughts, heroic gestures, and glamorous rituals could be challenged by a new and novel anthropological appropriation of the mundane and everyday.

For Husserl, assessing phenomena was not to engage in phenomenology—as it regrettably (and quite mistakenly) is for so many contemporary anthropologists. Once Husserl realized (as Sontag much later did for metaphor) the folly of pure empiricism, he reversed his focus, recognizing that meaning was meaningful only when hermeneutically embedded. This is why phenomenology, and especially existential phenomenology, soon found its home in literature and the arts and why reflexivity—as a theoretical practice—emerged not in ethnography, but in French literary criticism. As Heidegger would later claim, the words of poets constitute the house of language, and philosophers are the guardians of that house.

Indeed, those who have tried to strip meaning of its cultural content have failed repeatedly, whether they be ethnographers focused on objectivity, postmodernists focused on individual experience, or philosophers focused on perceived phenomena. Time and again we see that deep meaning is carried precisely in the collective social exchanges that fuel external object relations—what Mark Johnson calls the "nonpropositional and figurative structure of embodied imagination" (1987: xxxv; see also Napier 2003, 2004b). Acknowledging this truth points if anywhere to the need to see poetry, art, and ritual as the precise places where any social group will invest itself most thoroughly. However, if you have ever had the desire to host a nice party you will also understand why ritual and the ritualizing of objects really matter; for at such moments we, as Tylor well knew, invest ourselves in similar small rituals involving symbolically heightened object relations. This triangulation between persons, things, and social engagements is what Armstrong (1971) calls the *affecting presence*—an interior characteristic of an object that both accounts for its power and engenders unique affective social responses. In refining the opportunity to make meaning socially, we allow for the possibility of focused social meaning and also new growth. As Hecht and Simone so aptly put it in critiquing development (1994: 16–17):

> In their efforts to help, development workers forget, at times, that for the impoverished to survive from day to day they must ward off the hopeless reality that objectivity is constantly trying to impose upon them.

Citing an imam from Mali, they add (ibid.: 17):

> Change must discover unexpected reasons for its existence; it too, must be surprised at what it brings about. Only in the tension between the old and the new does the elaboration of a moral practice occur.

Of course, in art, music, dance, and ritual—that is, in so many nonnarrative places—these nonpropositional structures of embodied imagination lead to the invention of new moral practices. In such nonpropositional spaces, we discover socially and collectively new ways of reframing the hegemony of internationalized categories of meaning—be they diagnostic, humanitarian, or just plain colonial. When people manage to create new forms of empathic meaning they don't need to name them to feel their affects.

What Tylor sensed already well over a century ago was that the possibilities of what could be imagined by humankind could be profoundly evidenced in the extraordinary diversity of thought elaborated through collective agreement (i.e., through culture). He also was quite aware that the myopic nature of what his own society allowed to be defined as *religious* indicated a near total failure to elevate the senses to the natural status they universally occupy in what we now call embodied meaning. Indeed, Tylor would have found the contemporary, politically correct tendency to homogenize all of human emotional life demeaning, pretentious, and offensive. As he puts it adroitly (1913 [1871], 1: 479):

> The modern vulgar who ignore or repudiate the notion of ghosts of things, while retaining the notion of ghosts of persons, have fallen into a hybrid

state of opinion which has neither the logic of the savage nor of the civilized philosopher.

These were courageous words in both his era (which so often found very real "primitive" peoples to be subhuman and disposable) and ours (which finds it impossible, or unacceptable, to imagine moral worlds other than our own righteous ones).

Remarking the appearance of Hamlet's father as a fully armored ghost, Tylor develops a view of spirituality that is deeply phenomenal and culturally relative. Commenting on missionary accounts in North America, he offers multiple ethnographic (nearly universal) cases that exhibit how "souls are, as it were, the shadows and the animated images of the body, and it is by a consequence of this principle that [certain peoples] believe everything to be animated in the universe" (ibid.). In highly animistic settings, such immediate forms of connectedness—where all objects may be inhabited by sentient forces—allow humans to have an impact on the cosmos through ritual. And ritual, in turn, makes it possible to orchestrate one's local world symbolically, to develop concrete connections with one's immediate environment, to orchestrate innovative responses to moments of uncertainty, and, in short, to manage one's daily world creatively. At once, in other words, Tylor dispenses with what would one day become the crisis of postmodernity by taking seriously what Mauss (1935) later calls *les techniques du corps* (the techniques of the body). Animism was for Tylor a concrete, empirical way of relating bodily sensations to embodied meaning, embodied meaning to moral judgment, moral judgment to decision-making, and decision-making to action.

Indeed, combining animism with a local cosmography allowed, as Tylor demonstrates through countless examples, both for the concrete and direct orchestration of specific responses to uncertainty and, when focused on ritual, for the mechanical practices that made it possible to read local environmental and experiential signs for paranormal content. If, for instance, an animist applies beliefs about the auspicious or inauspicious nature of the cardinal points to various locations in the landscape, he or she has in place an operable mechanism for responding to, and possibly warding off, disaster.

Likewise, good intentions (the techniques of ritual and prayer) can compound positive outcomes by intensifying auspicious forms of embodiment. Balinese, for instance, can ward off ill health by appeasing minor spirits in the landscape and avoid major disaster through, as we noted, orienting homes and temples in auspicious directions. Once properly oriented, both harmonious feelings and the life force that carries them (*rasa or "feeling"*) can flow more directly to and from a relatively permeable body now tied directly to its environment (Napier 1986, Chapter 6).

Yet, in spite of so-called progress (or perhaps because of it) we are today obliged to discount what seemed remarkable to Tylor. The stigma against envisioning genuinely different notions of personhood is, if anything, exacerbated by global narratives about the uniformity—the universality—of psychological experience. Placing the self literally in other things and people both reshapes concepts of responsibility and implies that unique notions of the body might give way to culture-specific forms of emotional life. This is all well and good when such differences are not thought of in any hierarchical manner, but it is very dangerous when they are. Once it is acknowledged that a particular mode of culturally constructed selfhood could create unique skill sets, the idea that one culture might be better at one thing or another leads to a kind of biological determinism that frightens well-intentioned humanists into suppressing the uniqueness of local experience in favor of broad structural generalization. Suddenly, a fascination with creative difference is condemned by recasting it as a glamorization of the exotic. In so doing, the experiential baby, fragile though it may be, gets abruptly thrown out with the bathwater as the ethnographic rabbit runs for its bolt-hole.

But we do know in fact that body techniques can be learned and cultivated in exceedingly diverse ways, perforce developing unique forms of perception and unusual skill sets. It is what we call cultural learning: those who are good at it recruit allies and succeed; those who are less good fall to the wayside, are thrown out by the pack, or choose isolation if they can find it. Such ordering creates preferences and hierarchies ("we" become better or worse at something than "they" are)—the very stuff of social Darwinism (Napier 2004b: 20–22).

Universalism strikes us fearfully as the only viable choice, even for radical social thinkers. Michel Foucault's early view of personhood—in which the discursive practices of collectively oppressed people were subjected to the regimes of power that would have us all participating in our own subjugation—is one form of such universalizing about personhood and collective meaning across cultural domains. Though this draconian construction was revised in Foucault's later work on sexuality and desire (for after all what is animism if not an expression of sympathy and desire?), the idea that individual identity was largely subjected to regulation by the state and reflected in the actions of a compliant or resistant self was taken up by many of Foucault's admirers. As a result, human action became defined by social thinkers in more uniform, political terms than local, existential ones.

The humanistic assumptions about the need to cultivate some global uniformity around what constitutes a person (as we see not only in human rights discourse but in social theory [e.g., Butler 1991] may build on anthropology's diverse representations of what can constitute meaning for a person while still assuming a more monolithic and normative view of personhood itself. Though there is a long lineage (from Socrates to Fanon) theorizing about how people react to nations and states as hegemonic managers of what can be called meaningful, such universalizing concepts of perhaps better integrate into contemporary normalizing views of the person than into earlier ones that focused on the existential implications of diverse modes of thought (see, e.g., Leenhardt 1942). Indeed, reading colonial narratives—where "otherness" fascinated, but mostly scared the hell out of, colonizers—readily illustrates what has been erased by the mad desire to write in homogeneity across the entire human landscape.

What rings true today as much as yesterday is the fact that the ways in which a body and its image-boundary get constructed are more or less limitless. What is partible for some Melanesians may be connectible for some Indians, just as what is impermeable for a certain European may be permeable for certain Balinese who, quite happily, will describe the carrying away of an illness by shifting its pathos onto an inanimate thing that can be taken from one person and pressed on another for good or ill intent. The power of such modes of thinking—their unique significance for collectivities of people—is, then, evidenced each and every time we take the creative abilities of other modes of thought in any serious way.

Seeing the importance of ritual—as the dramatic and creative coalescence of forms of heightened social agreement—was not only what allowed anthropology in Tylor's day to rise as the core field in which alternative modes of thought became a real subject of investigation. The study of religion also made possible the birth of medical anthropology—particularly through the groundbreaking work of W. H. R. Rivers, a first-rate fieldworker and a founder of modern experimental psychology. In demonstrating the insightfulness of Rivers, it is worth quoting the first paragraph of his pioneering investigation in full (2001 [1924], 1):

Medicine, magic, and religion are abstract terms, each of which connotes a large group of social processes, processes by means of which mankind has come to regulate his behaviour towards the world around him. Among ourselves these three groups of process are more or less sharply marked off from one another. One has gone altogether into the background of our social life, while the other two form distinct social categories widely different from one another, and having few elements in common. If we survey mankind widely this distinction and separation do not exist. There are many peoples among whom the three sets of social process are so closely inter-related that the disentanglement of each from the rest is difficult or impossible; while there are yet other peoples among whom the social processes to which we give the name of Medicine can hardly be said to exist, so closely is man's attitude towards disease identical with that which he adopts towards other classes of natural phenomena.

The extraordinary power, diversity, and elegance of what modes of thought humans have come to invent cannot to this day (and despite our academic erasures) be underestimated. They are also evidenced each and every time we acknowledge the diversity of ways people conjure together to feel better or worse; and we gain little by simply calling such views regressive or antique. Far better, in fact, to accept their remarkable diversity and durability as evidence of a human capacity to produce forms of meaning that are as powerful as they are special. To know something of them, then, is not a luxury but a necessity of modern life; regrettably, the discounting of epistemological diversity is promoted by human rights activists and human rights abusers alike.

To claim, then, that the sympathetic animation of one's environment is a "primitive" (rather than another good) way of seeing the world is not only to reject as unknowable what we may not already know, but also to assume that it is somehow unnatural to us. Yet as Nicholas Humphrey shows in his wonderful work on medieval law, the legal prosecution in medieval courts not only of animals and insects but also of inanimate objects was done out of fearing the loss of control over the world and as a way of institutionalizing empathy (2002: 150–51):

What the Greeks and mediaeval Europeans had in common was a deep fear of lawlessness: not so much fear of laws being contravened, as the much worse fear that the world they lived in might not be a lawful place at all. A statue fell on a man out of the blue, a pig killed a baby while a mother was at Mass, swarms of locusts appeared from nowhere and devastated crops.

At first sight such misfortunes must have seemed to have no rhyme or reason to them.

As Humphreys points out, subjecting a block of wood to a criminal investigation (because it fell on, and killed, someone) seems not at all odd from
the level of believing that objects and the powers they embody are subjected to the same laws as those of the human world, and that the human
world, in turn, is moved by the same divine order that moves objects and
other foreign bodies. Any so-called atomic view of the world allows us
to see both that we are all swayed by the same energies that are in and of
everything and that these energies can be transferred in greater or lesser
degrees through sympathetic means.

To wit: any theory of unity demands that we believe that the world
around us is both connected and subjected to the same rules as we ourselves are; for (Humphrey 2002: 251)

> the natural universe, lawful as it may in fact have always been, was never
> in all respects self-evidently lawful. And people's need to believe that it
> was so, their faith in determinism, that everything was *not* permitted, that
> the centre *did* hold, had to be continually confirmed by the success of their
> attempts at explanation.

The stronger those connections, the more self-evident they became:

> So the law courts, on behalf of society, took matters into their own hands.
> Just as today, when things go unexplained, we expect the institutions of sci-
> ence to put facts on trial, I'd suggest the whole purpose of legal actions was
> to establish cognitive control. In other words, the job of the courts was to
> domesticate chaos, to impose order on a world of accidents—and specifi-
> cally to make sense of certain seemingly inexplicable events by *redefining*
> *them as crimes.* (ibid.: 251–52)

As Durkheim (1912) also knew well, animistic taboos that rely on sympathetic forms of magic to produce affective outcomes can have the same
preventive consequences on human behavior as presumably more advanced
forms of medical explanations in which the inexplicable is less defined as a
crime than as a clinical condition. In illness, that is, the threat of a dire consequence can function equally as a behavioral proscription and as an indicator
of chronic dysfunction, particularly when sociopathology evolves impercep-
tibly into physical or psychological morbidity. Deviance and medicalization

in this view serve the same purpose as once did the animist's sympathetic practices and taboos, even if once medicalized we treat the deviant (sociopath) and the patient (psychopath) in wholly different ways.

The practice of acknowledging abnormalities while accepting that we are all connected by whatever animates us became the basis for all systems of law (Maine 1861); for laws are what keep us in line and what provide us with good reasons for action when chaos invades life. But I would go further: if the apparently absurd legal actions that Humphrey describes were designed to gain cognitive control over chaos, they also depend on the idea that all of nature shares and traffics in some same controllable thing—that what is "of man" (as we used to say) is also of a pig, or a swarm of locusts, or a block of wood—and that it is controllable because it is shared and traded among us all. It constitutes as well as connects us.

So, being partible or permeable in certain cultural settings enhances our capacity to create meaningful connections (and sometimes formal obligations) locally, by reinforcing the belief that we are all subjected to the same natural energies and the laws that we create to control chaos formally. In addition, such interdependent and fluid ways of connecting to a local world can help build strong forms of environmental responsibility: to orchestrate symbolically and sympathetically; to develop concrete, immediate, and innovative responses in moments of uncertainty; and to apply them to the preservation of what we value locally. In animistic settings, fluid body image boundaries allow us to be creative in visceral ways that are less Cartesian; whereas in more Cartesian settings such fluidity is seen as regressive and as dangerous.

But can the creativity that made possible such alternative modes of thinking be learned? Here, the literature on creativity is telling, because unlikely combinations and superimpositions of things remain central to the process of invention (Rothenberg 1988). New ideas derive primarily through creative superimposition of mental images (literally of neural templates that are stimulated visually); and creative thoughts, in turn, are amplified by thinking while doing—that is, through physical activity (e.g., walking, dancing, hiking)—in short, by seeing the self in and through its behavioral landscape. Creativity, at least considered experientially, is an inventive, connective process enhanced by physical engagement, to the degree that its experimental domain may be dampened by Cartesian dualism or redirected into religious experiences that channel lived emotions into institutionalized practices (Csordas 1994). These formal tendencies are what led Tylor to think of monotheism as not just a natural extension of animism, but as a higher form of social engagement.

By contrast, the skillful animist is constantly experimenting with local meanings, engaging powerful symbols in local space, and building embodied practices out of empathic responses to visual and tactile stimuli. That is why animism goes hand in hand with divination; for divination is nothing if not the creative integration in space and time of powerful structures, empirically superimposed on place and space.

Divination has, therefore, great creative potential, attempting as it does to read natural signs and to ascertain cosmic conditions. Diviners are in this specific way unlike those who pray: they seek new understanding by manually organizing and interpreting concrete things of this world. Divination is a form of creative interpretation that is nourished and enhanced through empathy and contagion. It promotes the condensation of animated objects in the interest of forming new meaning: for seeing what has not yet been seen; for orchestrating chaos in the interest of discovery. Many highly creative people can be thought of, in this sense at least, as diviners.

As a transformational technique, one might even posit that the kind of cosmic reading made possible by divination—where the local environment is symbolically interpreted and acted upon—is progressively abandoned in monothetic and monotheistic abstraction. In monotheism the presence of an omniscient god makes divination obsolete. In the absence of physical connectedness monotheism induces chronic psychological liminality and attenuated and other-worldly forms of sentimental attachment. What might have been a direct, viscerally continuous ritual engagement for the animist is replaced by solipsistic uncertainty. A child having witnessed an accident may desire for years to become a medical doctor. In the interim he or she lives out again and again the unresolved and internalized moment of destabilization before seeing its uncertainty resolved ritually in the ceremony of becoming a physician.

Viewed ontologically, one can examine to good effect how psychoanalysis has rationalized the cultural desensitizing of the body, how it has restructured the meaning of desire, and how it has discounted what we loosely call animism as an infantile and regressive behavioral mode. To recast psychoanalysis and other such reflexive processes as apologies for the symbolic and visceral disunities of modernity (rather than as curative interventions), it is useful to examine how these very practices and beliefs had their origins in the explaining away of animistic behaviors made no longer socially valid by the modernist program. What was hysteria for Sigmund Freud and Josef Breuer if not the initial basis for Freud's theory of psychoanalysis made meaningful by the patient's (e.g., Anna O's) inability to link through narrative the destabilizing moment (the contagious psychic trauma) to some conscious explanatory structure? The impulsive emotionality of hysteria resulted, so Freud thought, from its inability to resolve itself over time. Its disconnection from life—its uncertain meaning in the social world of the patient—led to its being a catalyst for psychic pathology. Find a way of making the event consciously meaningful and, it was thought, the ongoing psychic disability might be transcended.

Seen as a rationalizing response to an unresolved sense of "being-in-the-world" (*Dasein*), to borrow an idea from Heidegger (1962), the psychoanalytic program is not at all unlike the modern process by which traumatic victims transcend their private horrors through therapeutic writing and verbal narration (Pennebaker 2003). Interpreted from the perspective of passage rites, one could argue that psychoanalysis is modernity's facilitator—even apologist—rather than its interpreter. Pathologizing what is uncertain and liminal allows for one also to pathologize the impulsive emotionality—the hysterical reaction—that characterized and catalyzed the patient's emotional connection to a visceral moment.

For psychoanalysis, then, much of what is wrong in the world of maladjusted body image boundary stems from the fetish and especially from the individual's unwillingness to relinquish it. Those of us who have allowed ourselves to be so swayed by objects in our environment are thus seen, in a psychoanalytic sense, as suffering from an inability to separate in a healthy manner the self from its behavioral world. Why not then acknowledge that such a separation creates the need for psychoanalysis in the first place?

One reason is simple prejudice: this being that to engage in animistic practices is regressive, an unhealthy pattern common only to children, so-called "primitive" peoples, and the mentally disturbed. In psychoanalytic terms, those who actively cultivate environmental relations by perceiving themselves more fluidly and symbiotically are not only engaging in regressive behavior that must be outgrown, but also risking through repetition the development of deep and damaging neurotic disturbances or psychotic episodes.

As Antze points out, Freud's early thoughts on illness treatment center on the process of storytelling. Storytelling builds meaning through constructing narratives of agency and its loss that

> follow the classic pattern for dramatic irony, in which the protagonist is shown to suffer from a kind of ignorance, a failure to see her real situation. And yet, as Freud repeatedly observes, there is something willful about this ignorance: "The hysterical patient's 'not knowing' was in fact a 'not wanting to know'—a not wanting which might be to a greater or lesser extent

conscious" (Freud and Breuer 1974 [1895]). The initial splitting that gives rise to symptoms is, he insists, "a deliberate and intentional one," usually driven by the wish to avoid a harsh truth or a difficult decision. "Thus, the mechanism which produces hysteria represents on the one hand an act of moral cowardice and on the other a defensive measure which is at the disposal of the ego" (ibid., 188 [Lambek and Antze 2004, 112]).

But Freud's early awareness that his psychic excavations read more like short stories might have led him down an entirely different road had he been positioned to develop an interest in Mauss and van Gennep (1909). The malingering and psychosexual obsessive compulsions that Freud came to associate with both hysteria and adolescence leave little space for the deep commitment, the eternal connection if you will, of the animist with his or her social and physical environment. A space so completely ruled by empathic desire and local responsiveness has no place in the modern world of psychic attenuation in which transformations are rarely immediate and both bodily and psychic growth are considered healthy only if one can always identify a body, a self, that is prior, persistent, and psychically consistent.

What is more vexing still, the space between local practices and universal diagnostic categories creates a logarithmic growth in possible new disorders in which all variation can be pathologized as dysfunctional aberrations of psychiatric norms. The animist—now removed from those carefully monitored spaces of empathic exchange—experiences a pain no less deep than the indigenous person removed from his or her dreamscape, place of ancestral connection, or shrine of animated fetishes. The success of psychoanalysis—as a widely adopted explanatory model rather than a frequently unsuccessful mode of curing—may, then, as easily be read as a testament to the true outcome of disjoining a person's life from its object of meaning as it might an explanatory model having the status of scientific fact.

But where Freud placed his bet on the ability of his system to cure through narrative excision the now dysfunctional animistic transformation, Jung perceived the more creative and positive dimensions of projection. After all, what is the construct of the *collective unconscious* other than a statement about how we connect with things-in-themselves? And what is a thing-in-itself, to return to the first pages of this book—if not a mechanism for the retrieval and creative reshaping of a disturbing personal moment within a shared and not fully known collective space? What is the thing-in-itself if not a device through which a troubled person can refashion him- or herself? Remember what Bernini, the great Baroque sculptor, once said of art: the greatest works of creative expression are realized not through completely independent thought but through making something beautiful out of the flaw—that out of place thing-in-itself.

In fact, the greatest works of art, he felt, were those that addressed a flaw (a pathology if you will) in such a manner so as not only to make it the center of the new artwork but also so central that the work could not have existed without that flaw (Napier 1992). Indeed, much of the Counter-Reformation in which Bernini lived and thrived was built in greater or lesser degrees on the belief that lavish works of art and architecture were necessary for the resurrection, revivification, and recreation of primordial objects in yet more empathically compelling form. The job of Counter-Reformational thinkers, in other words, was not to reject the past or what was different, but to show how the past's imperfections could be perfected and interacted with physically—to reshape the flaws of what has existed in a former time or that exist in another tradition into something more beautiful and remarkable still. Read this way, the Catholic response to Martin Luther was the battle cry of the Counter-Reformation: the role of humankind is to take God's work and reanimate it through art.

But the higher you fly, the harder you fall. Tap into these psychic depths of human experience and you may also find yourself "chosen" to do for others, as every shaman knows, what neither others nor their societies can do for themselves. Jung's fascination with the Book of Job and with the alchemical *coniunctio* are vivid examples of his personal response to having felt it his destiny to reframe humanity's psychological relationship with its experiential world.

Was Jung's sense of having a mission an illness or a gift? Perhaps the point is moot: a person can never know in advance of succeeding or failing if the extraordinary commitment required to learn things genuinely new will be viewed as delusional or superhuman. The outcome cannot be known in advance, which is why the prior and persistent self must be sacrificed in helping others do what what they seem not able to do for themselves. The Holy Grail, the thing-in-itself, is thus the device for acknowledging the truth of a person's developmental uncertainty. As von Eschenbach already shows in his twelfth-century *Parzivaal*, this uncertain thing—this Grail—must be the object-of-objects on which is inscribed the charge that "any Templar chosen by god's hand to rule over a foreign folk must refuse the asking of his name and help them to their rights."

Choosing or being chosen, that is, to seek out the thing-in-itself is a deeply religious task, carrying with it the possibility not only of creating something very new, but also of risking destruction and failure. Note, as did Mauss, with what trepidation and feelings of nausea and ill-health a

Trobriander must accept a powerful kula object from a trading partner. Note in particular the requirement that trading partners make good on the exchange by bringing yet more fame to the animated objects they receive, and one senses immediately the burden of creativity—that is, why those who reanimate the things we collectively share may suffer deeply in so doing. This may well be what Nietzsche had in mind when he described humankind as being doomed to create.

To conclude, if auto-narrative and therapeutic writing are viewed as modern curative processes in which a body seeks out its own continuity through storytelling, what can we learn from the desirous commitments of the animistic, regressive, body? Are there places in modernity where Tylor's challenge and charge that we think beyond culture can be realized—where we learn from others new ways of taking responsibility for the local worlds we inhabit?

Or is it only the awareness of what we have lost that we gain by reconsidering what animism makes possible? And if only this, how do we come to grips with the depth of pain caused when an animist's local symbolic world is disrupted, when the Australian or Native American is forced to relocate in the interest of progress? How can such a daunting task be accomplished when it also requires one literally to lose one's consciousness into the things of this world?

Finally, does the creative possibility inherent in animism—its concrete ritual focus on local meaning—offer us any insight into what it is we seek to recover and reshape when we look longingly at traditional systems of knowledge? Can animism assist us by informing our desire to connect locally in ways that are more than cerebral? The opportunity is there if only we will acknowledge it.

PRACTICUM 4 | Assessing Cognitive Diversity

As the world, for better or worse, becomes a global community, the diversity in modes of thought that once proliferated has also decreased radically. If one considers how languages embody categories of thinking—how this book, for instance, may represent only a handful of those ways of thinking—the real threat to cognitive diversity posed by language loss (as a reflection of cultural loss) is staggering.

Though numbers of existing languages can only be guessed at, it is widely agreed that about half of the roughly 7,000 languages currently spoken will disappear before the end of this century. More horrifying is that roughly eighty of those languages that have a global presence account for the languages spoken by some 80% of the world's population; the remaining 6,900 or so ways of thinking still there to be examined are held by only about 20% of the world's population. And the figures get worse by the day, as these threatened ways of speaking, thinking, and understanding disappear at the rate of one every fortnight. Of the roughly 6,800 so-called living languages (i.e., languages that have enough speakers for dynamic forms of communication to take place), around 90% are spoken by fewer than 100,000 people.

While we remain quite aware of the problems relating to loss of genetic and biological diversity, cognitive loss is another matter. Many foundations support endangered species, while others promote the revival of dying agricultural practices or help store and circulate endangered seed varieties. But linguistic and cognitive diversities are different: the human mind is restricted in its inability to be aware of what it does not know, including what it no longer knows. Ignorance of what is lost at the level of conceptual diversity is thus more than bliss; it is a loss of being able to ask how diverse ways of giving meaning to things can actually provide us with novel models for addressing old problems. The problem of ignorance remains that "you do not know what you do not know."

For this reason alone, a fuller understanding of what forms of environmental behavior are possible is critical, even if such understanding requires an extraordinary commitment; for what we lose in this regard cannot by definition be obvious. Many serious questions are raised by the loss of cognitive and conceptual diversity. Here are but a final few that may be of assistance in sensing just how enormous such a loss actually is:

1) What are the social barriers to developing new forms of environmental connectedness? How can a person stay put long enough today even to consider investing locally rather than globally?
2) How have our systems of capitalization limited our willingness to take important objects out of those systems of exchange in which they are invariably commodified?
3) What are the psychological pressures that apply to our not animating things around us? Why are those who animate their local worlds so often considered regressive, infantile, or even ill?
4) What might it take to record and understand even a small fraction of the ways of thinking that can be environmentally embodied in unique categories of thought and in the languages used to define and express those categories?
5) What in your own view might encourage you to give priority to local meaning and to stay put and work through what is required to enrich your own life and the lives of those around you?
6) And finally, what might encourage others to join you in this effort?

EPILOGUE

1. Personal Challenges

It would be inappropriate to conclude this book without some reflection on the difficulties presented to a contemporary reader in taking seriously the arguments and recommendations made herein. Creating meaning through ritualizing local objects is not only potentially troubling psychologically but also requires us to ask what it is about contemporary life that makes doing this especially challenging.

In this final section I will not provide ready answers, but I will describe some of my personal struggles with the very tasks I have set out for readers. I do this not so much to explain why I have designed the challenges the way I have, or to show through my own experiences only how attempts at making deeper meaning can be thwarted by outstanding social norms and practices. I do this rather to show how looking for what cannot be known fully is often arduous but also fulfilling.

I begin, therefore, with a brief reflection on making symbolic meaning in my place of residence and move on to discuss the hurdles any reader must overcome to invest symbolically in his or her immediate environment. Finally, I discuss the psychological obstacles that challenged my identity as a creator of symbolic objects—that is, as a craftsperson and artist.

———————

Thirty years ago I acquired a house in a beautiful setting in rural Vermont. It was a relatively small home that had been originally built to

126

last by a state senator in the 1820s, but now sadly in shambles. People thought it a somewhat insane idea: beautiful though the location was, the structure was literally collapsing. The wooden sills on which my home stood were rotten around its entire perimeter; every pane of glass in the large barn (several hundred) needed to be glazed and reframed; many were broken. The barn roof was partially blown off by various storms, and there were pigeons everywhere. A few weeks after moving in, I got onto the roof of this new home to look for the source of a leak. Leaning against the chimney as I climbed up, I thought I felt it move. I pushed a bit and watched in horror as many tons of brick—the entire chimney!—fell into the front yard.

What was worse, the interior was not original at all, having been remuddled over the years with whatever was lying about. The kitchen had at least four forms of flooring; the wiring throughout the house had been recycled from the barn after a previous owner had given up on dairy farming, and I was shocked by stray electricity on water pipes many times as a consequence. Wild animals moved in and out of the building freely, as did the real estate agent who only nodded anxiously when she came around, as if to say, "Why did you do this?"

So when I got my monthly paycheck as a young, college lecturer, I had to make and remake on every payday the same decision: be financially clever and put my meager extra money into a market-dependent account that (at that time) would grow exponentially, or buy more supplies to keep the endless building projects resourced. After a few years of opting for the latter, I realized that what I did made enormous emotional sense to me but was financially destructive. Money spent on wood and cement was, for all intents and purposes, money lost—unless we sold out, which was hardly the reason for investing blood and sweat.

Paradoxically, the more I realized what I was doing, the more I did it; because I knew that were I actually to be defeated to the point of financial disaster there would be a wealthy stock investor with windfall profits waiting to spend his or her earnings on my beautiful home once I could no longer afford it. I had to make this work, and that thought disturbed and frustrated me—especially the idea that the extent of my work could never be known to that smart holiday home buyer who would happily relieve me of my burden for whatever price he or she could negotiate.

Soon enough, I realized I could only be in this project for the long haul. I began to accept that my goal was not to spruce the house up, to pass it on, and to reinvest my profits—what developers call flipping a property. I had engaged in building to learn about each and every board so that at some future time my descendents would be able to be proud of what I did.

In short, I had become dangerously immersed in trying to make my local world a better place.

Because my capital was no longer fluid, I was running against what all financially successful people preach—namely, that it is foolish to locate your assets in immovable property. The smart guy pays no allegiance at any local level unless doing so is advantageous in the short term. Even political leaders were now preaching the free trade gospel, inviting others to follow them in giving up on local allegiances: put your money elsewhere; avoid taxes at all cost; maximize your profits. It's the American way, after all, but a way that would once have been considered quite unpatriotic—a word deriving from the fatherland (*patria*) practices of Romans who legally tied voting rights to land ownership and local investment.

Indeed, already in the Middle Ages, migrants—Jews and Romany, in particular but also Muslims in the East—were at times held in suspicion not only because they were less stationary (even though their migrations were so often forced upon them) but also because trading and money lending (the kinds of work left to them) could bear interest. Money lenders made money at night while they slept. To increase one's earnings while sleeping rather than through the hard work of one's hands was considered immoral by many medieval Christians, even if Calvinism eventually taught some Europeans to think otherwise.

Because capital by definition must turn every physical investment of labor into a measurable and exchangeable commodity, medieval money handlers were often scorned by those who invested body, soul, blisters, and personal injuries in the hard labor of learning a craft—not only because earnings could be accumulated around the clock by those who gave loans, but also because, as many West African Muslim traders are so fond of saying, "money has no smell" (Stoller 2002). In contrast, for many medieval Christians the sacred nature of craftsmanship was often emphasized. Guilds and freemasons over the centuries created mystery cults out of the secret knowledge of building, as if some basic human urge to make locally meaningful objects transcended capital; for everyone knew that work not done to the highest standard would reflect badly on local forms of meaning and hence on the quality of local life.

The notion occurs in many traditions around the word, but for medieval builders there could be no inferior work done neighbor to neighbor, such mediocrity being left for those early globalizers in the Age of Discovery who went abroad to exchange trinkets for precious resources. Indeed, this awareness of craft is an ancient one having ramifications far beyond an individual's or group's beliefs about material meaning.

Local often used to trump global: in Teutonic law, for instance, one's word spoken directly to an exchange partner—that is, locally and face to face—constituted the making and completing of a contract. Signing a document as proof of agreement was secondary, a practice still reflected today in German marriage law where one is considered legally married as soon as one takes the verbal oath, not when people register their commitment to one another by signing a document in the town hall. What you do in the presence of another—how you behave in your local physical space—was, and yet sometimes still is, much more important in establishing and maintaining trust than signing legal documents.

But the consequences of investing in the local physical world would run deeper still in Europe, and far after the Middle Ages. When Martin Luther accused the Catholic Church of losing its spirituality in its apparently decadent overinvestment in material wealth, the Church of Rome responded, as we noted earlier, with the Counter-Reformation. Its entire thrust was to argue that, because the Catholic faith revived and refined ancient spiritual archetypes, it was its *obligation* to make the world a more beautiful place through architecture and art. As Pope Alexander VII said when he nearly bankrupted the Vatican to build Bernini's piazza in front of St. Peter's Basilica: "Nothing may be done in honor of the Mother of God unless it be something great." These very words are inscribed in Latin on the pediment of this famous piazza (Napier 1992).

There are serious and deep questions we need to ask ourselves, then, if we decide to make the things around us into more than simple commodities:

Is being committed locally a self-destructive act in the increasingly globalized context of free trade?

Are we actually today being fiscally irresponsible by loving the place we inhabit?

Would I have been better off forgetting that my love of home was sentimental—better off thinking of my own self-interest instead of about what used to be called community?

Well, the obvious answer to all of these questions in a country dying to reject its own *patria* was, of course, a resounding yes. To think that calculating politicians who abandon local investment in the interest of free trade could become serious candidates for high office made me realize just how archaic the place of *things* had become in the contemporary world. Indeed, how to change that trend for the better now challenges us to the core as global forces worked very much against local investment.

2. Handwerk

I think about local meaning as I now write while riding on a train through central and southern Germany: Fulda, Wurzburg, Nuremberg, Munich. And I think especially about how the cultivation of superior skills for local purposes and forms of meaning creates investments of empathy and time that are very vulnerable to global processes—investments that, in turn, can lead both to a local binding to place and to fears of the potential destabilizing effects of things foreign on local forms of reciprocity. Such sentiments had their most negative impact in Germany in the 1930s, and they also led Jews after WWII to desire fiercely their own fatherland.

But I am reminded by being here on this train of another ethos regarding local physical investment. In spring 1987 I was invited to the Johns Hopkins University to participate in the launching of a new program in anthropology and art. During a weekend trip to rural Virginia, on a local notice board I saw posted a photo advertising an eighteenth-century clothing cupboard (a *schrank*) for sale that was clearly not of American manufacture. To make a longer story short, I was intrigued enough to ring the number provided.

The following day I negotiated a quite fair price for the cupboard, rented a trailer, and returned to the previous owner's home where we dismantled the rather large piece of furniture for transport. As we did this he pointed out a very small, nearly illegible, message written on one of its inside panels. Upon reaching my home in Vermont I used a magnifier to read the faded message. It conveyed the fact that this *schrank* had been made in 1749 by Johan Caspar Schmid of Unterlenningen, a small town outside Tübingen in southern Germany, as his masterpiece, had been submitted to the local guild, and had been judged as evidence of his qualification for entry as a fully accomplished cabinetmaker. This piece, in other words, was his *masterpiece*—a demonstration of his complete control of the skills and techniques necessary to be admitted into the regional guild. What it said was this:

> Johan Caspar Schmid
> gebürtig in Unterleningen
> habe diesen Casten zu meinem
> Meister Stück gemacht alhier
> In Eßlingen 1749.
> (I, Johan Caspar Schmid,
> born in Unterleningen,

have made this wardrobe,
my Masterpiece here
in Esslingen, 1749.)

In addition to being fascinated by finding this testament to the meaning of the elaborate nature of its construction, the statement alerted me to a widely noted work ethic of this region of Germany—an ethic for which it had become famous throughout Europe, and eventually the world, in promoting the highest levels of technical skills. Even today one can find across this and other parts of Germany aspiring craftsman engaged in their journeymen's years (*auf der Walz sein*), traveling on foot and in ancient dress from one location to another in search of specific skills from various masters. For reasons of training, my *schrank* too, I discovered, looked much more like a piece of furniture from fifty or one hundred years earlier than its date of manufacture, it being important that the applicant to the guild demonstrate his knowledge of known and well-established construction techniques. From apprentice to journeyman he could then himself become a master craftsman by submitting a masterpiece for judgment that showed his knowledge and manual skills to their fullest. My *schrank* was just such statement of skill.

This tradition not only gave rise to Germany's fame for producing fine craftsmen, but later also led to the migration of craftsmen during the Industrial Revolution, especially to the United States where skilled German artisans were valued highly in American industry. In fact, such training has from medieval times indicated the mastery of an art, the term being applied equally to the art of making and the crafting skill necessary to realize an idea.

In my hometown of Pittsburgh, Pennsylvania, for example, Andrew Carnegie (Scottish steel baron and library philanthropist) launched the Carnegie Technical Schools (now Carnegie Mellon University) with the notion that successful industrialists should also be skilled draftsmen. The original buildings were designed with sloped floors so that classrooms could be modified easily to accommodate the ever changing mechanical and drafting needs of budding industrialists: because Carnegie recognized the connection between design and production skills, the university has evolved today as a center of excellence both for the finer arts of painting and music on one hand and for computer sciences and robotics on the other. As scholars often say, Carnegie Mellon University today somewhat resembles a rather odd combination of the Massachusetts Institute for Technology and the Julliard School of Music.

In other words, what we see is the outcome of Carnegie's belief that a well-trained industrialist should be a person of practical applied skills—a draftsman who could draw an idea, accurately translate that idea into an object, and then become a user of that object who not only understood its inner workings, but also could make something better because of that understanding. Now, one has only to compare such sentiments with the knowledge base of today's computer user: someone who may know something of programming but little or nothing of what makes the computer function, a person for whom the tool used daily is nothing more than a mysterious black box.

By contrast, so-called patternmakers of Carnegie's day were highly valued for having exactly such comprehensive skills, often using—as did Schmid—simple hand tools to convert raw wood into the finest forms. Unlike the computer programmer of today, Schmid created by making a machine that would allow for some new, third thing—the product. Thus, it is from this ancient tradition of Handwerk that our notion of master of arts derives—the academic distinction originating in a deep-rooted notion that being a master craftsman in an academic discipline requires mastering one's art.

What these educational priorities indicate, in other words, is a strong connection between thinking with one's hands and creating finer objects—objects that in their best forms would be fetishized by those who made them, those who used them, those who sometimes consecrated them, and those who would come to see the best of them as irreplaceable. Thus, putting yourself into your work could become a veritable religion for guild members whose secret knowledge of a trade was often quite carefully guarded. Pride in work and pride of place were, for the skilled craftsman, essential aspects of making the world one inhabited concretely better. At the height of wealth and fame, Henry Ford, for instance, was no happier than when working on an old tractor or accompanying his friend, Thomas Edison, in search of one or another original machine.

Today, as these manual skills fade, so do the opportunities for understanding in an embodied manner the environmental importance of such modes of thought and action. But the sentiments are not wholly lost, even though recovery will be difficult and trying—both because of the effort required to transcend modern prejudices and because of the psychological demands made on us when we tie ourselves deliberately to the making of meaning through things around us.

So, yes, when I build, I build as if the place will be somehow connected eternally to my efforts. This is not pretentious fantasy; it is simply acknowledging if I commit myself to creating symbolic meaning in a particular location, that my effort becomes a part of the history of the place—a history that gets created and recreated spiritually—because doing this, as it were, ritually includes acknowledging a certain affective truth. And that truth is one of imperfection, mistakes, and potential redemption. Not redemption of a canonically religious kind, but in the sense that what I have done has engaged, if imperfectly at least recursively, some element of the earth's finite resources in a way that makes me more conscious, even momentarily, of my privileges and obligations—a kind of transcendent recycling.

3. A New Psychology? Dangers and Prospects

But surely the most trying challenge of living with things in an era where local meaning may be quite literally devalued—where exported selfish interest is erroneously meant to produce its own moral system of exchange—is that of taking real, concrete steps to rethink one's identity in local terms: to reconnect with the environments we inhabit. For such a person a service economy is, as mentioned earlier, a slave economy.

Though this book is only a small gesture in the direction of rethinking this problem—one of many possible patterns for establishing ritual relations with one's local moral world—its demands on one's psychic self may run deep. Its apparently light provocations, that is, may be potentially disturbing, and there is no way of getting around the fact that the animation of one's environment and the making of complex symbolic object relations that accompany such animating practices can be destabilizing psychologically.

This danger I can profess to know perhaps better than I would like to admit, not only in the aforementioned ways I troubled over my personal built environment, but also in the ways those actions precipitated a serious challenge to the Enlightenment notions of body and soul that I had been previously acculturated to value via my Catholic upbringing. Indeed, in the Middle Ages the Church of Rome already fretted, as noted earlier, whenever local attention to shrines and holy saints distracted worshippers from devotions that focused on God the Father and towards a mere local saint with whom they might more readily communicate.

So much was omniscience thought imperative that the Church would claim as early as the sixth century that the Pope, as God's representative on Earth, was infallible. Even the secularizing of identity during the Enlightenment did little to alter the affect of that monotheistic legacy on the way that an individual made meaning with the physical world: the mind of the rational person may have replaced the soul of the faithful believer as the locus of human transcendence, but in no way did the notion of personal identity alter to accommodate more deeply one's built environment. In fact, in many ways personal identity became even more fixated on autonomy, transcendence, intellectual genius, and personal accomplishment—the foundations for what we may now see as the truly neoliberal person.

Thus, for me, this challenge of thinking more environmentally—of being more defined by experiences and what they make one into than by my self as a prior and persistent entity—took the form of a deliberate destabilizing of my identity as a practicing artist; for in the creation of meaningful things, symbolic objects (paintings and sculptures, in this case) readily replaced words as expressions of local meaning. Handwerk, as it were, became a substitute form of communicating.

This transition from talking to making is central to what artists do. Take Pablo Picasso, for instance, the world-renown artist we discussed briefly in the Preface to this book. In my view he was not a terribly great inventor, but he was a great *bricoleur*—a person having great skills that he applied to the inventions of others. Picasso is often described as a "giant" by ego-oriented historians of art; though he actually did much better at standing on the shoulders of giants. Above all, Picasso had a keen sense of how unlikely objects might be combined, and he devoted himself tirelessly to making highly symbolic things (that is, "Art") by hand. Not being a writer, or much prone to eloquent speech, Picasso responded to nearly all of his emotional impulses, for better or worse, through the creation of paintings, sculptures, and collages. He spoke with his hands, and it was this practice of extending himself into the world through making things that compelled him to create feverishly.

But more recent artists have abandoned these practices, often having their work fabricated by others and denying deliberately the referential or psychologically representative nature of what they create. However, because Picasso and many of his era maintained a strong interest in converting social and emotional sentiments into acts of art making, they also often aspired to become better portrait artists who could capture the soul of a subject in expressive gestures—the act of making portraits being throughout time centered on an artist's impressions of his or her subject— a *What-do-I-think-of-you?* activity in which the artist reflects on and somehow represents a subject or client. In this model of social interaction, gifted artists interpret subjects, capturing essential elements that somehow stand for individuals and their experiences.

Because of the high challenge of creating successful portraiture, this interpretive art rose as perhaps the most supreme form of symbolic object making and the greatest of all artistic challenges—a fact understood long ago when Christian iconoclasts argued against the creation of holy portraits (because they presumed knowledge of God) and still throughout the Islamic world where images are so often prohibited for precisely the same reasons.

This capturing process implicitly acknowledges the idea that an artist's gift resides in the understanding of how to express what subjects either do not understand of themselves or cannot manage to capture (as portrait artists are meant to)—an essence, that is, of a personality in a single image. Portrait artists in this way work to interpret and represent some presumed existential reality that their artistic gifts permit them uniquely to see and speak of. Good artists capture their subjects or moments in their subjects' lives that are somehow especially meaningful.

In this way portraits have always been, at the level of identity, past oriented; they stand as artifacts of what is or has been and as evidence of the artist's seeking and capturing skills. Because of the portrait's extraordinary potential, many subjects shy away from having portraits painted of themselves or portrait photographs taken. Indeed, the feeling of having been captured is so strong that those unfamiliar with the tools of representation are sometimes wary of them. Anthropologists have widely evidenced reticence and fear among isolated groups of a camera's ability to capture souls or bring back the dead. Those who like being photographed or painted are, conversely, often accused of plain vanity. In fact, the seeking and capturing aspects of portraiture are so powerful that the act of making them is replete with hunting metaphors. To cite one common example, photographers not only take pictures but also shoot them—the genius and skill of artists being measured by the extent to which critics and viewers judge photographers' hunting skills.

This awareness—that a portrait gallery can sometimes resemble a trophy room—is not new. On occasion, artists have tried to transcend these identity hunting (searching and capturing) practices through either making subjects anonymous or deliberately focusing on the surfaces rather than the essences of portraits—the depersonalized portrait somehow achieving a more universal meaning without individualizing its content.

A stunning example of this more generic practice can be evidenced in W. Eugene Smith's haunting photographs of Midwest industrial workers in the 1950s. Fleeing the fashion world of New York photography, Smith came to Pittsburgh intent on capturing everyday people. He sought to create a Homeric vision of industrialization and deliberately selected a location where he could concentrate on what to some was, as Charles Dickens famously called Pittsburgh, "hell with the lid off."

There are, of course, many such examples where images of real but anonymous people are put forward to represent grand themes, where capturing practices represent civilizations rather than individuals—where individuals, in turn, stand in for essential universal experiences that are transcendental. The point being that anonymous portraiture remains one strong technique for attending to image not ego.

The other way of undermining the ability of a portrait to represent individuality is, of course, to question the validity of representation itself. Here, capturing practices are transcended through a clever exploration of superficial similarities in which a search for so-called inner reality (the soul of the subject) is replaced by an attention to a surface form. Arcimboldo's famous sixteenth-century portraits—in which the surface features of a subject are replaced by various objects—is one good example (Napier 1992). Another similar but more targeted practice was Salvador Dali's so-called paranoid critical method in which dream worlds are brought to life through an attempt visually to read two surface meanings at once—a portrait of Mae West, for instance, becoming simultaneously a representation of a living room and furniture. Here the search for the essence of West is replaced by the visual and frightening psychic experiences that Dali's deliberate and obsessive narcissism made possible (ibid.).

Though there are other ways in which artists de-individuate their subjects, these three show some primary techniques by which artists have challenged the relation between surface and essence and the artist's role in achieving control over presumed inner realities. What should be noted, however, is how these de-individuating processes—in objectively revising and condensing complex experiences—*ritualize*, as it were, complex relations in a single image. Smith elevated individuals by giving them epic roles; Arcimboldo toyed with the superficiality of identity as a way of alluding to rituals of display; and Dali showed how personal ritual (his own art-making) could itself be psychically deceiving—where Narcissus (now, for Dali, also a hand) looks so gloriously and deeply into the reflective pool that he falls in and drowns in his own infatuation.

But even in these cases the image, as a past-oriented assessment of something prior and persistent, has remained a largely unchallenged practice throughout the history of the representational arts. In fact, this is concretely what representing implies: some evaluating and assessing procedure in which what is or was gets fed back to us through the eyes of a sensitive interpreter whose own prior and persistent artistic self we also glorify when we attribute fine works to particular people who make and sign them. What has been very much missing in these attempts is, I would argue, the creative dimensions of ritual activity: how the enhanced symbolic nature of a thing redefines an old identity in a new and even novel manner; how artists, more profoundly, can be true to their work by becoming what their work transforms them into.

4. The Captured Artist

In 1970 I went to the University of Leuven to study phenomenology. There were not many places in the world to do this at that time, and in the United States only a few courses of study were available at places like Duquesne and Northwestern. As a young artist in a new and foreign place, I soon bumped into not only other young artists but also older ones who had (literally) run from Hitler's trains with their artwork in their arms. One of my philosophy teachers, in fact, had brought the archives of the great phenomenologist Edmund Husserl out of Germany hidden in a horse-drawn cart, and the memory of the war was close enough that many valued their freedom of expression as much as life itself. Often they ignored art criticism, and, when they did not ignore it, they usually had little good to say of it.

The artists I met were true bohemians. They had studied with well-known painters and sculptors in Paris. One even was old enough to have been the student of the Flemish father of surrealism, James Ensor, whose small portrait of himself in 1960 (a lithograph of a reclining skeleton completed in 1888–1898!) stands out famously as an ironic and sarcastic comment on the superficiality of portraiture and on a portrait artist's inability to capture the so-called inner reality of his subject.

Across the ocean in North America, the art world of the early 1970s was, if anything, dominated not so much by artists as by their critics. American artists, especially, had at that moment abandoned the idea that artists could themselves or through images represent something called *reality*. Both representational and expressionistic forms of art had long been left behind for minimalism, in which representation itself was rejected, or super-realism, in which hyperreal paintings signaled the arrival of a matrix world in which art could outdo life.

But showing that a camera could "see" more than the human eye might, or removing all illusions from an artwork so that viewers are forced to stop seeing one thing in another, appear in hindsight rather literal, if not reactionary, attempts to innovate. Both minimalism and super-realism were less inventive than they were innovative attempts to demystify illusion. Interpretation was no longer an artist's prerogative, having already been given over to art critics of the 1950s and 1960s who made and broke artist's careers and even their lives.

But as a twenty-year-old troubled by what was taking place in New York, I quite happily got to know both a bit about phenomenology and a dying bohemianism that somehow still flourished in a few European local traditions. Neoexpressionism (now quite common) had not yet emerged globally, so what I witnessed in these pockets of European tradition fascinated me. Before I knew it I was brought into this group, most of whose members were thirty to fifty years my senior, and in the following year I had my first one-person show that sold a good bit of what I had made in the intervening months.

Though all of this excitement left me quite hopeful to imagine what creative possibilities painting might hold, my immediate (if modest) successes also alerted me at a rather young age to something many artists work for decades before realizing—namely, that success is a huge identity trap. Already in that first year it occurred to me that I was quickly being identified by the particular expressionistic style I had developed. The realization came in two forms.

The first was the fixating of my name by my clients—the result of what seemed then a coincidence but actually now seems a key part of my destiny. When I began to make things as a student, my initial attempts were in figure drawing and ceramic sculpture. In making ceramics, applying a signature to often small objects made of dense clay was awkward, often disturbing if not wholly ruining the piece or at least making one's name far too obvious. So, instead of signing works, I adopted a sign—one as important to logarithms as my ancestral surname. Rather than trying to write "Napier" in clay, I used a double pi sign. There have been entire books written about the meaning and function of pi, but the double pi is a fractal, that is, what a mathematician would call a nonterminating irrational number. I quite liked the implicit irony.

This practice of identifying myself in my work with a symbol rather than a signature meant that as soon as I began to sell my paintings, collages,

and constructions clients began asking me to sign my work—something
I had already put aside. The requests raised my concern. Why, I thought,
should I be forced to sign work? Are my clients unhappy that I sign them
symbolically? Are they, now like so many museum goers, already looking
at the label before looking at the work? Are they thinking, "Do I know that
name?" "Is this piece worth spending time with?"

Second, because I worked so often in diverse mixed media, clients also
wanted to see me through the style they felt they had invested in: like much
better-known artists, I was already aware (fortunately at such a young
age) that I was being defined by what I made and how it characteristically
looked. I came to realize, in other words, why so many well-known artists
made more and more of the same things they had already been identified
by—not only (as supporters and critics argued) because they were refining
a private, visual language of expression that had its own unique vocabu-
lary; but also because clients often took notice of anomalous work and
rejected its difference. "Do you have another piece like the one I sold to
such-and-such a client," the dealers would sometimes inquire? What I was
being asked, in ritual terms, was to repeat—with the same outcome—an
acknowledged form of symbolic meaning. Looking around, I saw how
many well-known artists had fallen prey to fame: the better known they
became, the less freedom they had to rethink themselves.

In response, I began to engage in my own version of identity decon-
struction. Like a modern-day graffiti tagger, I stuck to my symbolic signing and sometimes made and left art anonymously in public places. I also
diversified my style of expression and intentionally mixed media to the
degree that my last commercial show, in Brussels in 1977, was reviled by
one critic as a "one-man group show." Like Bernini, who sculpted himself in 1623–24 as the biblical David, I too began to see my audience as
an identity-devouring monster. Over time, I found myself resisting capture—making anonymous what fulfilled me creatively and ritualizing my
engagement with each artwork I created.

In fact, my last show consisted of a mere dozen works—each of which
was reworked from a previous piece and again reworked, sometimes
repeatedly, after the exhibition. Each autonomous piece had, like a young
human cell, evolved in a particular way—committing itself to a pattern
of growth, finding itself in some very new place, even if not necessarily
identified as a work of art, let alone a work of my art.

At the time, I remained unaware that my interest in collage was based
on some strong psychological evidence about creativity. Later I would
realize (following discussion with a Harvard psychologist who studied

creative processes) that the superimposing of unlikely things—the making of visual collage—was the basis for most forms of discovery, sustaining unlikely superimpositions until new forms emerged.

This collage making was a thing I had been trained for from infancy as a subject in Benjamin Spock's experimental nursery school, when I was given by his assistant, Margaret MacFarland, my own room—my own studio—to construct imaginary things and talk about what I saw in my creations. My artwork always was a kind of collage making, a superimposing of media, of second and third dimensions, of forms of representation and abstraction, even of everyday practice.

Though some would have (by the time I launched my one-man-group show) identified my rather radical view of myself as professional self-destruction, the act of resisting capture demanded that I think about other things—specifically about my own identity; about the affect of others on my identity; and about the creation of ritualized engagements in social space. Mad? Perhaps. Engaging? Absolutely!

People would tell me I was "different"; because, now, I grew tired of the solipsistic nature of art making and of the psychological isolation in which artists produced what they made. I had seen how isolation could make one exceedingly creative while also making other forms of communication virtually impossible. I had also seen how my reworking over and over of the same works would mean that the only way a work could ever be finished would be when someone bought, stole, or by whatever means removed the piece from the ontological horizons of my imagination—when the creative ritual, that is, came to a conclusion. I realized that I was developing with each new piece a systematic form of engagement in which the work became the locus of complex ongoing symbolic relations. I was creating a series of fetishes.

Alone, preparing for a new show, I sometimes lost my ability to speak in coherent sentences. I fell wholly into the very works I was making and both loved and hated the intense places I had created. I consigned months of work to galleries only to forget where the works were. I gave an entire year's work to a dealer only to discover later that he had flown a private unregistered plane to a nearby airport, that he would claim never to have taken the pieces, and that he later would fail to pay for anything he had consigned. My psychological ambivalence about the art world grew daily. In a way, I was becoming an increasingly bad artist!

At the same time, the so-called international art market seemed much more provincial than it purported to be. I wearied of the odd claims of the organizers of international exhibitions that there was something global or universal about the art industry and the artists who had enslaved themselves to it. I yearned for the use of art objects in making local meaning. Galleries and clients differed significantly from country to country—even in venues that claimed to be international. I realized that I did not want to be any gallery's artist, that if I were ever to enjoy the act of making things I would need both to engage myself in other modes of thought (even uncomfortably alien ones) and to consider how I might engage others in the processes of creation—where the sum of the effort of two people could become greater than the individual parts each independently contributed.

5. Rethinking Ritual Engagement

Eventually, I came to see that I was better off making other sorts of art, or maybe of making artfulness a way of life rather than a way of making a living. I mean this in the literal rather than the poetic sense, for I was by now impatient with art as artifice—no more galleries please, and thank you very much, no more retrospective or memorial shows. No more self-important artists signing works; just me and my place of work—then, a rural barn—to somehow try making holy. I had witnessed and studied precisely such practices in South and Southeast Asia, and it seemed natural to me to abandon the grotesquely commercialized art world completely.

So I exchanged a brush for builder's tools. It was a good but also a very dark time. A friend asked me for a curriculum vitae, and instead I sent a single page—only later to discover that I had been nominated for a prestigious award (which of course I did not receive). The president of another major foundation devoted to celebrating youthful creativity invited me personally to apply for their well-known award. I never answered the letter. It wasn't that I did not desperately want the freedom these forms of recognition could provide. It was more the trap I felt they represented. Besides, there were, no doubt, so many others who would (and did) gladly take that stage and make better use of it.

In response, I became more and more professionally homeless. I just could not accept that these gestures of support were as free as they appeared. And besides, I was quite tired of being asked what I would do next—almost as an insult, as if my restlessness would keep me from ever becoming serious about anything.

And under such a cloudy sky, what do you do? You do what you think is right. You just go away and find something that brings a bit of joy to life. That's where both anthropology and homebuilding came in. I traveled when I could and lived abroad, but while at home I built—two hundred sheets of plasterboard, six hundred panes of glass. I lost count (and a good part of my lungs), but the losing count made so much sense in this dark place I then inhabited. Throwing the die in a sacred cave in Bhutan made so much more sense than chatting up art merchants in New York or in Dusseldorf.

By my mid-twenties I had the great fortune of becoming a student of anthropology at a British university. The fortune was not only that of discovering anthropology, but also of doing so at a time when UK universities still supported eccentrics. I soon discovered that at Oxford I was free to think that gallery painting and sculpture were more or less irrelevant—a great relief to one who found the pretentiousness of it all rather agonizing. Unlike in Belgium, France, and Germany, there was little everyday interest in art in the United Kingdom. What interest there was at the time seemed to replicate national patriotic ideals: one sculptor (Henry Moore); one painter (David Hockney); and a host of other quite poor would-be important people, unless they were dead, of course, in which case there would be lots of retrospective shows for them (Bacon, and so on). I could almost hear the pasty critical discussion: Let's see, which already known artist will get recycled for this new season? Which self-consciously new talent will be discovered? Golly, I can't wait! Sounds just like every other season—over and over and over again.

6. A Buddhist Long Fast (3 decades, 3 years, 3 months, 3 days, 3 hours, 3 minutes)

But one of the advantages of having devoted myself to remaking art for my private purposes—even allowing it to become something else entirely— was that it liberated me to focus more on the transitional spaces between the isolation of the studio and the social spaces in which others made meaning of what I did. I thought, and at times wrote, more and more about ritual. No longer being a professional also liberated me to enjoy sometimes just being bad at trying a new thing.

Modern-day neuroscience has now argued that we grow biologically as we make meaning socially: we become empathic, that is, through the so-called mirror neurons we each create as an emotional reaction to another person's expressed emotions. Our biological lives, in other words, also grow through emotional encounters with others. This kind of discerning tells us something important about the effects of ritual on biology: focusing wholly on the self can produce unique ways of thinking, but not unique ways that are reciprocal, let alone communicable, within the social worlds we inhabit. Perhaps this is why we look at art sacredly and without any direct physical response. Perhaps this is why when we go to a museum or gallery we gaze at things made by supposedly exceptional people—geniuses, we call them—who often work under conditions of extreme stress, isolation, and profound alienation.

The minimalist's rejection of personal or emotional involvement (where someone else literally makes what you think up) and the surrealist's glorification of self-indulgence (where, as with Dali, artistic identity is elevated to the point of divine insanity) both depend on some acknowledgment of the artistic personality as key to a work's creation. In this sense, though they seem miles apart, both yet promote very traditional, Cartesian views of personhood in which the problem of personal involvement is addressed through rejection or indulgence, but never through challenging the importance of names and identities. Artists failed to escape critics who strove to capture creative identity and seal it up; artists signed on, as Picasso admitted, because they could not remain outside and somehow be central to a formal art establishment.

From the standpoint of identity politics, one can make a strong statement: the established art world has gone nowhere since Picasso and company experimented with anonymity. The graffiti tagger got hunted down and domesticated in the gallery, as did those (like Banksy) who made a profession of self-mystification, of tagging, of marking and running. The game of hide-and-seek between artists and viewers got superficially reshaped, but never really challenged—or at least so it seemed to me.

The question of the self as a thing made by ritual experience, rather than (or in addition to) something only prior and persistent, was one that I first took up academically in my doctoral training at Oxford and in my first book (*Masks, Transformation, and Paradox*, 1986). Because the mask is literally a visage or faux portrait—a lens on the face—it *reveals* only when identity is socially created (as a *persona*) and *conceals* when a prior and persistent identity gets suppressed behind it. The great anthropologist Gregory Bateson told me that if I were to write about masks I had first to grow a beard (which I did), and my dissertation supervisor, Rodney Needham, advised me to bring a mask to my dissertation defense (which I also did).

But this paradoxical nature of the mask was not only something I took an academic interest in (following my deliberate unwinding of my artistic identity); it was also a condition of living that I had known from childhood, when, as Spock's three-year-old subject I not only got that studio, but also was daily placed in his nursery school panopticon—a school whose walls were all made of one-way mirrors (masks, as it were) from behind which our infant persons were scrutinized by teams of psychologists.

Though the environment of Spock's school could easily be construed as psychologically unsettling, if not wholly violent and violating, the experience of being educated there also had its informative dimensions. Years later it became clear to me—in my transition from artist to anthropologist—that I was being guided by a similar understanding: namely, that even when artists invite their subjects to participate in creating artworks, the artist will always involve the subject in the artist's own hypersolipsistic self-reflecting so long as the self remained a prior and persistent thing demanding analysis, a name, and the subject's appropriation. Artists are, in other words, rarely positioned to acknowledge how they get undone and remade by their encounters with their subjects—unless, like some performance artists they intentionally punish themselves as an art form. No one, in other words, applauds an artist's acceptance of the limitations of his or her own will.

So I wrote a few additional essays about this identity mongering that later, wearing an anthropologist's hat, I published in a book called *Foreign Bodies*. The problem of artistic identity was, I felt, further muddled by the fact that no one was prepared actually to ask in any serious way just why there had to be an art world at all. How could there be an argument for art if there was no serious counterargument about its uselessness? Oddly, most curators recognized the problem indirectly: too many big paintings and sculptures all by the same people, filling up the storerooms of museums and galleries, whose mission turned from engaging the public to regurgitating the same names from their vaults. Like an energy company squeezing the last resources out of a nonrenewable environment, the art world seemed to engage in its own excavation and mining operations. Open an art magazine at the dawn of the twenty-first century, and it looked much the same as it might have in 1970.

Having departed from that world of galleries and artists (who either loved or hated the art world but nonetheless defined themselves in it), I yearned for what the Germans call *fernweh*—a longing for being in an unknown place. I spent a year or so in Indonesia and another in India and made several trips to Nepal and elsewhere, looking at how people from various cultures used what are called art objects for other purposes. I was the first anthropologist to be allowed into Bhutan on a visa as an anthropologist. I wrote some books about so-called art along the way and thought more and more about what the philosopher Paul Ricoeur had described to my more attentive classmates at Leuven as *Oneself as Another*. I spent many years wandering among the homeless of the world, looking at how they engaged in their own forms of creativity, and I made films collaboratively about life on the street, about seeing oneself through others, and about creative processes.

In short, I did my best to erase my artistic identity. My art had not gone underground; oddly it had emerged as something else. And along the way a number of new creative forms got experimented with.

7. Autogeny

Many people helped me along the way, but in 1977 a man appeared in the form of my dissertation examiner who pushed me to redefine what I was doing. His name was Francis Huxley. He was thirty years my senior and had grown up listening to his father and his Uncle Aldous talk across the garden table with the likes of Bertrand Russell and D. H. Lawrence. He was a friend and colleague of R. D. Laing (with whom he shared his London flat at the time), had been a great experimenter with altered states of consciousness, and had written a book about another ancestral family friend, Lewis Carroll. Francis Huxley, too, wanted to look back through the looking glass.

Through many long hours of talk and years of corresponding with him my desire to make art differently emerged experimentally, while I continued making collaborative videos with the homeless. By the mid-1980s I asked Francis if he would be interested in creating another kind of art in which we would share responsibility for what was created. The idea I had was to make a portrait that was actually in large measure generated by the subject. Because I had long before become weary of the artist-hunter capturing images and impressions of subjects, I asked Francis to send me a photograph of himself that was taken by someone else. I wanted more to fuel a transformation than possess it. He went to a studio and had a formal portrait taken, which he sent me by post. We agreed on a plan.

I drew the portrait (one level of abstraction) and then divided it into forty-two equal pieces (the number 42 [6 × 7], according to Francis, had been considered magical by Lewis Carroll). Each of the forty-two individual abstractions was then photocopied repeatedly until it became unrecognizable as part of the original portrait. These pieces I then sent him one by one. He reflected on them over a few months and returned several with corresponding thoughts and pictures: a deserted beach on the Baja Peninsula; a photograph of his London apartment after a subletter had set it on fire; a poem. Each of his reflections provided a catalyst for me to respond to. I replaced original sections of his image with my reflections on his responses. In so doing, the portrait became not an activity by which I, the artist, would capture and hang like a trophy his preexisting identity but a forward-seeking version of a possibility—a possibility of becoming, a transformation.

The portrait of Francis became self-generated. We therefore called the project the Autogenous Mystery. But like my one-man-group-show there was no plan for completion. The project never ended—or rather, because it was infinite, it never could be finished. Francis and I lost touch for a time. Then one day a few years later, I was invited to attend the opening of a film festival for Soviet filmmakers who had been released from prison or house arrest following the fall of the Berlin wall and the break-up of the Soviet Republic. As one of Mikhail Gorbachev's gestures toward an open society, he had begun inviting artists to Moscow—Yoko Ono, the ex-patriate American author, Gore Vidal, and many others. At the same time he for the first time allowed Soviet dissident filmmakers to tour the United States as a gesture of open goodwill. The wall was coming down in more than a literal way.

Following the viewing of two films by the Soviet dissident filmmaker Kira Muratova, I was introduced to this Romanian-born artist at the customary reception. A friend of mine had been film curator at the Museum of Modern Art in New York and had arranged the event. One of her film clips previewed earlier that day involved handicapped actors in a churchyard (*Among Grey Stones*); the other (*Wide World*) was a love story between laborers building a banal new housing settlement. My friend, the curator, applauded the complexity of the second film. I interrupted saying I thought it was quite simple; it was about how people make love out of nothing.

The filmmaker turned to me and in a severe voice asked my name. "What do you do?" she asked. I told her I had been an artist but now was an anthropologist, that I had become interested in the uses of what we call art objects in other societies, and that I wanted to create a different sort of art that was less identity focused. She asked if she could see what I had created. I told her it was in storage. She asked if I could retrieve it. I said I could. She told her host that she wanted to cancel her evening appointments so she could visit my home. I went back to the farm where I lived and dug some works out of storage. When she arrived a few hours later I showed her several works and then described the Autogenous Mystery. When I explained what it was, she said the portrait was like a script for a film. Her eyes filled.

The moment stuck enigmatically with me: should I make yet a different kind of art? Had I not simply abandoned my obligations? I spoke to filmmaker friends. Bob Gardner, the well-known ethnographer who had worked among other places in New Guinea and in India, told me (in these years before video) I could do film but I needed money—lots of it. I got the message.

Meanwhile, I continued working with the homeless. Within that decade video appeared as an inexpensive medium; by its end I had coedited enough video (with my then-student collaborator Paul Dionne) to consider creating an autogenous video self-portrait—this time not by rebuilding images on paper or canvas, but through a series of nine separate films running simultaneously over a picture of my face. Later, I co-made a dual portrait with a homeless man I had known for some years in which our faces were superimposed as we spoke, morphing his African-Irish features with my Sicilian, Scottish, Polish, Alsatian ones. And I advised a student-painter about how she might make her own autogenous portrait out of landscape images that resembled facial parts—a modern-day Arcimboldo!

But again, my work entered the attic, remained unfinished, or disappeared entirely. Some work could not be made public because a collaborator wished to remain anonymous or for psychological reasons could not give informed consent. I made overtures around other projects—inviting the remarkable Parisian Czech poet and collage artist Jiří Kolář to create response pieces to a collaborative initiative I began about artists' masked self-portraits. (He sent me two lovely works, one of which became the cover of my book *Foreign Bodies*.) But my own portrait project sat gathering dust while I wrote of other things—the notion of the person in other cultures, ritual performance and personal transformation, the body as a medium of expression.

I built an *art car* with car artist, David Best, and a large crowd of enthusiastic bystanders after repeating in the donor car a cross-country journey I made in 1965. Then in 2009, almost two decades after my last gallery show, I was invited to give a talk at an exhibition at the Slade in London on art and the brain. I declined to talk but instead did a performance in which I showed my own video self-portrait, took responses by email for a week, and then did another spontaneous performance at the closing of the exhibition—a talk, an engagement with the audience, not a performance as something watched by them solely.

The experience of emerging again in a gallery was not entirely satisfying, but I did learn something from this rather vulnerable exercise in self-exposure. First, it became clear to me that only members of the audience who had invested themselves in the interaction were positioned in the end of the event to learn much from it. They had become a part of the ritual process, but one that was also polluted by the casual involvement of a wider audience of curiosity seekers. It was also polluted by the "art" label itself. The intimacy and fragility—the danger—of becoming was a thing too volatile for casual reactions. The only performance that could be constructive became the one in which the participants created their own interactive roles and then lived them.

I imagined a film in which this interactive process itself created new people who then represented themselves in the process—not a naïve, science fiction, or matrix world, but one in which life itself became coextensive with the art by which life was lived. Here the mutual reflection on new identity would create not altered states but new art, which in turn would create new story lines, which in turn might create other realities. I recalled Francis Huxley's fascination with Carroll's *Sylvie and Bruno Concluded*, in which mapmakers find themselves creating ever larger maps. In their search for accuracy they finally make a 1:1 map. Nothing is reduced when the symbolic and real are totally coextensive. In Carroll's absurd parody, the overlap is complete: if used, the 1:1 map would cover the country and render it dark. Realizing the dilemma, farmers instead used the country itself as its own map, which, Carroll assured readers, "does nearly as well."

In this sense, the problem of virtual worlds—the problem by which technicians try to replace physical space without ever reengaging it—could be transcended. The work became not a second life in which the engagement of art as a virtual space tried to replace daily living, but a third space in which a liminal transcendence—a rite of passage, if you will—could be completed in a new physical form. All of the messy wires and gadgetry of art technology—film, monitors, video, cables, chargers, computers, buttons, and greasy plastic keyboards—could finally give way to things one could (and might want actually to) touch, smell, and even taste when, as it were, one uses the countryside as its own map.

Such new work, I began to see, made it possible to enjoy life rather than simply replace life with a fictive and wholly imagined construct. Like the weaving of a Navajo blanket—where words spoken into the blanket as it is woven recreate primordial archetypes in new and novel ways—the work itself became an emphatic artifact of the creative process. Now, finally, after some thirty-five years of experimenting I could see what needed to be done and how to engage a work to completion. I could awake from a very long fast.

This new art was and is, an art of reciprocity—at once creative, therapeutic, nonsolipsistic, and hopefully inventive. Yes, the work became mine in that I took responsibility for it; but I also was now as much a participant, a facilitator, as I was a sole creator. The exercise became neither shamanic (in the sense that a shaman does for others what they cannot do for themselves) nor psychoanalytic (in the sense that the work would demand psychic excavation or exposure). What it had, though, was potential—the potential (not the requirement) to be either or both. As a reciprocal enterprise, the creation could become as private or as public as the engagement with an individual subject warranted.

Art worlds, art galleries, and art critics are now neither here nor there in my work. They are usable and useful but not much relevant. The artwork had become something no longer exhausted in itself, a form of incompletion, a potential rather than a commodity. At the same time, of course, my identity was also challenged in its traditional sense, for seeing oneself defined in one's connection to others through things-in-themselves required the abandonment of the egocentric self-promoting heroics so central to fame and the elevation of the individual as a self-motivated creator.

But what of creativity? If art were to be no longer attributable to identifiable genius, what kind of person would take the responsibility of carrying it forward? And what of the idea of genius itself?

8. No More Einsteins?

As an academic on leave in Switzerland in 2011, I had the luxury of awaking in the morning and looking out over Minusio, the Italian–Swiss village that first hosted the great novelist Herman Hesse after he moved to Ticino in 1919. Doing so brought to mind his famous novella, *Siddhartha,* about the search for spirituality in ancient India, and made me reflect on how the book's popularity only skyrocketed half a century later when translated into English for self-styled British and American soul searchers of the 1960s and 1970s.

Ironically, this powerful little book was anything but the celebration of Buddhism so many took it for. Attentive readers know that the novella was actually a critical reflection on what Hesse felt to be Buddhism's flawed doctrine of salvation—the doctrine embraced by those more Protestant Buddhists of the West who sanctimoniously aspired to follow in *Siddhartha*'s footsteps, toting the slim volume around like a hitchhiker's sign to anyplace but here.

As he died in 1962, Hesse fortunately was spared this embarrassing misuse of his work, and now, another half a century on, it is worth remembering that the book was actually intended to show us allegorically how creative outcomes are so often inhibited by our very determination to achieve them. Hesse's protagonist, Siddhartha, ultimately succeeds not through his own epic quest, but through the otherwise ritual act of ferrying other travellers back and forth across a river—an easy metaphor for what creativity theorist Edward de Bono calls lateral thinking and a wonderful metaphor for engaging the world in an anonymous, creative ritual.

In his now famous *New Think* of 1967, de Bono describes methods for learning how not to be enslaved by step-by-step approaches to solving problems along life's journey. Though de Bono offers (in this and other publications) concrete steps for casting off debilitating linear assumptions, the crucial point is that I can't find something I have not thought of if the process I employ tells me only what I already suspect. To this truth one might add an important caveat: if I have to show in advance to some auditor what deliverables my research will provide, there is no way that my work will take me laterally across domains of knowledge to a new place I have never visited—a place, anyway, that some impact assessor would have challenged my right to approach in the first place.

This obsession with finding what we are looking for is also why we so often mistake innovation for invention. Innovators are anything but inventors: innovators offer deliverables because their focus is on taking something already known and improving it. They engage in what we earlier on referred to as reverse engineering: Japanese and Korean manufacturers did not invent the car or the computer, but arguably they sometimes now design them a whole lot better than the rest of the world. Getting funding for innovation is relatively easy: the demonstrably better mousetrap saves money and delivers more dead vermin.

But if one remembers that just over a century ago the world's greatest thinkers uniformly agreed that one of the biggest problems of the future would be the accumulation of horse manure, caused by the transportation needs of a ballooning population, one can see how unimaginative we are in predicting genuinely new things and their effects on how we live. That's one major reason why only 3% of all inventions deemed new and useful by experienced patent reviewers ever see a profit for their inventors. The remaining 97% are either out there waiting for time itself to catch up or, like Hesse's novella, taken up by the wrong people and put to some inferior if not wholly inappropriate use. New and useful things also languish because they're ignored: it's hard to find patronage for what others cannot imagine. 3M saw no use for a glue that did not really stick until employees discovered how useful Post-It notes could be after an inventor left them lying about the place.

That morning, as I took a long look across the valley at Minusio and around the studio in which I worked, I was reminded of yet another great inventor, Thomas Edison, who once famously said that to create one needed to have both "a good imagination and a pile of junk." For Edison, the pile of junk was not an annoyance—some waste to be recycled—but a morass of imagined, lateral possibilities, a collage of relationships waiting to be seen in a new way. That aforementioned literature on creativity shows not only how important it is for a creator to engage ritually what at first may appear ambiguous—to keep ferrying passengers, as it were—but also how important having a pile of junk is to creating new things, providing as it does the superimposed structures used by a good *bricoleur* to discover the unlikely combinations necessary for producing something genuinely new.

This need for repetition in the face of ambiguity may explain why outcome-driven funders so infrequently support important discoveries; how could they when the methods they promote directly undermine what we already know about nourishing creativity? Limiting freedom of thought may itself be our best weapon against moving intuitions forward.

Is it any wonder then that so little comes out of a government's or charity's increasing demands that we remove the pile of junk, make better use of the wasted space it occupies, and punish any would-be Edison for having inefficiently squandered our precious resources? How can we expect genius to emerge from sponsored research? Well, under the current terms of engagement, let's face it: genius can't emerge because the ritual engagement with the pile of junk has no time to grow—the experiments outlined in this book being prohibited from the get-go. Full stop.

9. Diagonal Thinking

Some four-and-a-half centuries ago a distant member of my Scottish clan invented something called logarithms and with them the first analog calculating device—the predecessor to the slide rule we all used until digital calculators showed up. John Napier invented both logarithms and what has been called our first computer through lateral—or in his case diagonal—thinking: place columns of numbers side by side, read obliquely across them, and, presto, they calculate. The machine was called Napier's bones, and it took him decades of looking at numbers in parallel, lateral, and diagonal columns to arrive at a conclusion so simple that nobody could imagine how it hadn't been already discovered. We also got from him some other now essential things, like the first systematic use of the decimal point in base 10 and a range of other ideas we now find useless. (His own era most loved him for his attacks on the papacy and his use of the Book of Revelations to predict an apocalypse that would end the world by the dawn of the eighteenth century.)

Lesson learned? No uncounted time for imagining, no logarithms; no logarithms, no rapid navigating; no rapid navigating, no naval superiority; no naval superiority, no exploration; no exploration, no empire; no empire, no global dominance. It is not a legacy I should be much proud of perhaps, but then neither was John Napier in the end all that proud. In fact, he was so fearful of the military misuses of his inventions that he had evidence of their potential applications for weaponry destroyed before he died. At least, unlike Hesse, he anticipated what might come of certain of his creations were his apocalypse predictions to fail, as they did.

Apart from being doggedly tenacious and rather eccentric, what enabled John Napier to think up both so many useful and useless ideas? The answer here is simple: Napier was not only wealthy and eccentric; he, like Edison, was sponsored—in Napier's case not by the Industrial Revolution or by the Gates Foundation, but as the 8th Laird of Merchiston by his own peasantry. Personal resources gave him the time to let his imagination work again and again over the daunting accumulation of numbers (junk to the linear bean counters of his day). He had his rituals, and he repeated them faithfully. Junk needs time: some decades after Napier, the great Baroque sculptor Bernini used his liberal sponsorship by the papacy, as we have seen, also to make time for the unexpected to happen: as he put it, not to make something beautiful but to make an apparent flaw so much the centrepiece of a new work of art that one could not imagine it without that imperfection—in other words, the piece of junk.

Today, as our neoliberal governments attack education's free spaces, sell off the last of our hard-earned collective resources to cook their bookkeeping, and promise yet more of what Donald Rumsfeld might have called undelivered deliverables, one must wonder if Keynes wasn't right when he labeled such government cutting the *paradox of thrift*. Keynes argued that, in times of economic crisis and private fiscal reticence, governments should increase, not decrease, their deficit investments in the public sector; otherwise there can be no universities or other imaginative spaces where some discoverer named Albert Einstein might wander around in his bedroom slippers asking strangers to help him find his way across the next river: to find ways, that is, of letting his imagination wander; of visually superimposing one thing on another as he explored the landscape; of making something new by combining two unlikely things into a third that is greater than the sum of the two parts—in short, of behaving ritually to create and to procreate in the interest of making things better.

Fame is the spur that the clear spirit doth raise (That last infirmity
of noble mind)

—MILTON, Lycidas 70–71

AS WE FIND OUR way to the end of this brief experiential endeavor, I would like to take just a few moments to say why I believe that public anthropology, and your participation in it, is so important. I also want to make the case before concluding this brief exercise that the new forms of technological innovation have, as Michael Fischer (2003) argues, really shifted the social domains in which each and every one of us can participate to some good effect in the social order of things.

If the days aren't yet gone when people in power (including academics) function as gatekeepers between average citizens and indigenous peoples, they are in my view quickly coming to an end. What follows here is a brief warning to my anthropological colleagues, to self-proclaimed advocates, and especially to those advocates who allow themselves to be heroically described by others. It is a challenge that I have made in two other publications, but that I believe has a special meaning in the context of the growth of public anthropology.

I have taken the liberty of quoting Mark Twain earlier in this book, but now he warns us about hubris and vanity: speaking of our tendency to dwell on ourselves, Twain once claimed that the first duty of every human being is "to think about himself until he has exhausted the subject, then he is in a condition to take up minor interests and think of other people." Twain's sarcasm was directed against the crude self-interest that for him defined humankind, but he could have been talking about the reflexive entrapments of contemporary anthropology in which the process of validating the authenticity of one's experiences leads to an obsession with the self. Like Narcissus, we anthropologists on occasion project other voices as our own without knowing how much we depend on our appropriating the sensational moments, the extreme experiences, of the peoples with whom we work. While we question how other fields represent their subjects, we anthropologists are never so entranced than when we successfully convince our readers of the depth of our experiences. This we do not only by describing life in the field, but also by claiming that our narratives give voice to others or, more bluntly, by just laying claim to another's sensory world. As a result, some of the adjectives used to describe how we give voice are kind on ethnographers but others are not.

Such appropriating is, if anything, worsened by what otherwise seem to be laudable practices. Protecting the anonymity of our subjects can, as we have seen, exacerbate our evangelical inclinations when "their" anonymity gives way to "our" visibility. And when we advocates become chaperones or ushers by marshalling other people into public view, our behavior can border on flamboyance. In the worst cases, advocates who make much of voice-giving are received with caution for their clamoring because it may not always be possible to separate the words of anonymous subjects from the heroic delusions of the anthropological voice giver. This is why the chaperoning of those we study often goes hand in hand with shepherding—with the exhibiting and parading of others in public places.

Because of the degree and kind of control that the giving of voice can require, Bill Nichols (1981) once compared ethnography to pornography: both are highly inauthentic in their structuring of affect; both manipulate what we are allowed to acknowledge as psychologically relevant; and both depend on an expository realism in which the interpreter becomes sole controller of the space between the distanced observer and the (now objectified) person observed. And anthropologists, like pornographers, also succeed or fail by their ability to hold hostage a viewing audience—to make others participate in the view of the other being displayed and scrutinized. This is why anthropologists are at pains to inform readers that they are in the know, which is one important reason that giving voice is central to various forms of professional brinkmanship.

Setting aside the undignified squabbling over experience that sometimes occurs, it is clear that ethnographers are often at their most insecure when upstaged by the experiences of fellow anthropologists in the trenches or when denied access to a social space occupied by a colleague who may claim to know exclusively some indigenous view. Confronted with experiential domains beyond our personal knowledge, we are left with two alternatives: (1) remain silent in the face of the extraordinary (which, by the way, is also why those engaged in true life-and-death struggles so rarely write award-winning books about them); or (2) assimilate what we observe of the experiences of others as aspects of our own heroic quest.

So the problems of representation are multiplied, not lessened, when advocates give voice: subjects become vulnerable to ethnographic fantasy; authors have to validate themselves publicly and repeatedly; shepherds must learn ventriloquy; and institutions are compelled to validate immortalized winners with promotions and awards. Finally, altars on which subjects are either consecrated or sacrificed must be stabilized through cohesive networks that bind loyal allies into contracts of silence, for who will dare challenge the heroic good guy? In all of these activities one's subjects become victims of whatever trope the ethnographer has decided to exploit, while potential critics are silenced by the evangelical circumstance through which someone gets saved. It's just bad form to challenge a hero, even if we know that he's exaggerating wildly. This is why those who describe the tragedies of others can basically say what they want: no one would dare unwind such moral entitlements when the lives of others are at risk.

Because of what stakeholders stand to gain or lose, a central problem with advocacy is that it encourages anthropologists and their subjects to merge in ways that may be understood quite differently by each party—to merge, by having, as it were, elaborate courting rituals but never simple personal relations. This problem applies to participant–observation in any form. However, it is most obvious when ethnographers cannot comprehend another worldview. In moments of profound ignorance we are unusually tempted to valorize not only our subjects' narratives but also our own. And because vulnerability is not a thing we can verify at a distance, the claim that one is ameliorating it is not contestable. Human rights work, therefore, is often the place where appropriation borders on vulgarity. It is also, for the same reason, the place where the problems posed by diverse modes of thinking are consistently played down. Ethnic clashes in Rwanda provided a case in point: media followers were paralyzed by graphic displays of brutality during which moments advocates seized moral capital. Abusiveness is always a charge of which one is innocent and others guilty. Show me, that is, a person who is not when asked an advocate for human rights.

However, even where diverse cosmologies or religious beliefs are openly acknowledged, we see time and again how participant–observation can become the catalyst for unexpected encounters whenever writers describe native conflicts in which they participate. Among anthropologists, Paul Stoller (Stoller and Olkes 1989) finds that the death of his sorcerer-mentor leads to familial anger over privileged information the deceased is believed to have imparted to the ethnographer. And in the popular literature on cultural travel (where calamity is the norm), David Abram (1984–85) discovers that his magical tricks are no entertainment for Balinese healers who decide to respond to his extraordinary displays with serious and threatening attacks of their own. Blame Abram's plight on not being an anthropologist, but the recent controversy over Napoleon Chagnon's work among the Yanomami (Borofsky 2005) reminds us that long-term experience is no safeguard against the pitfalls of being placed squarely between those without voice and an audience hungry for hero epic.

When ethnography leads to undesirable outcomes, only rarely will ethnographers do as Stoller does and describe those circumstances in a noncongratulatory fashion that is constructive and open. More commonly, the result bears an eerie similarity to the psychopathology known as Munchausen by Proxy syndrome (MBPS), a form of mimicry in which it is not Baron von Munchausen's famous feigning of clinical symptoms that is replicated, but the feigning of sympathy by the very individual who induces an illness in another. The person with MBPS gets someone else sick to participate in a self-valorizing play of passion. Is the parallel with ethnographic misadventure a fair one?

I suspect we'd all say it's fair when the outcome involves people getting hurt. But what about when the difference between an ethnographer's worldview and that of his or her subjects results not in physical harm but in catastrophic ignorance? What do we do when the anthropological shepherd finds himself on stage with a flock of subjects who actually are not there to sing the choral chant in his private dramatic performance? This happened, for instance, with some advocates of the Kayapó—like The Body Shop, Cultural Survival, and a number of famous anthropologists we will not name.

What do we do about advocacy when worldviews and expectations end up being so different that the apparent consensus between advocates and those for whom they advocate is not at all what it seems? The Balinese call this *magic by wrong address* because misaligned intentions cause magical spells to ricochet and strike unwary people nearby (Wikan 1990), just as the anthropologist-gone-native can fuel misconstrued expectations and displace local powers in unexpected ways. Like the initially positive reception of American soldiers in Iraq, the indigenous embracing of our anthropological Captain Cooke may not presage the favorable outcome it at first appears to indicate—especially when an anthropologist is encouraged by his discipline to take as his first duty the description of his own feelings.

In spite of evidence to the contrary, some will still argue that smart people don't make these big mistakes—that is, that such errors of judgment are made by lesser men and women who haven't studied anthropology. However, the better-known anthropologists among us also nonetheless manage to destroy themselves professionally (by inadvertently stepping into in the wrong roles); for academic networkers must cross various cultural chasms whose bridges are vulnerable, and many who regularly make those crossings in broad daylight are subject to fire that is often unfriendly. Leave those Honduran peasants long enough to speak at that Amnesty conference, and return to find that local militias have rewarded them with an Almighty vacation. Without singling out Honduras, there is a reason why it is sometimes considered the most violent country on earth. Ferry between presidential offices, major funders, fickle philanthropists, and the miseries of the oppressed, and an advocate will eventually (and surely) know disaster. Risk so much without putting on a good performance for the media at that same Amnesty conference, and not only endanger those left behind in the bush, but also fail to legitimate your agenda under the bright lights.

The central problem with advocacy is, without putting too fine a point on it, that the chances of positive outcomes for our subjects may actually *decrease* as an advocate's visibility *increases*. This is one important reason that human subjects committees are gun-shy when it comes to having graduate students and their professors work in politically sensitive places. It's also why the Peace Corps traditionally would have nothing to do with applicants holding degrees in our field. So there is a paradox here that cannot be overstated: anthropologists have made laying claim to being "outside" a prerequisite for membership in our professional collective. One's group membership is predicated, that is, on denying what group membership requires.

Now, remaining inside by convincing others that you are outside is a time-honored practice not only in anthropology but also in contemporary life in general, which is why the "writing of passage" has become an academic industry involving university departments, institutional overheads on grants for researchers who advocate, and forms of self-promotion that border on the ludicrous. Like bohemian artists, winners in the advocacy race have always been those who can best convince others that they are not a part of the system while at the same time dipping very deeply into institutional networks of authority. We all know this to be happening before our eyes, but we haven't said much about it because, without alternatives, doing so seems too damaging. Call attention to the experiential pulpit-pounding of every do-gooder who lives to become a household word, and you simply empower more indolence among a general public already fatigued and depressed—until recently at least because today's systems of communication have made possible new relationships that transcend the mediating roles of many who once stood between indigenous peoples and outsiders.

Today, our understanding of the degree to which anthropologists have functioned not only as advocates but also as gatekeepers in their own right is enhanced when we witness the results of employing new mechanisms that allow students to leapfrog over gates rather than pass through them. It is not only corrupt local governments, politicians, warlords, and scoundrels, that is, who have distanced indigenous peoples from the outside world; those same peoples have also been distanced by hierarchically inclined anthropologists who have kept others out as much as invite them in—a fact that, of course, could not have been known before the appearance of new ways of communicating that now already seem common. Not knowing, in other words, is problematic; not knowing what you do not know is, to yet again paraphrase Donald Rumsfeld, more problematic still.

But now even my undergraduates, and those of you who have with seriousness and determination pursued the suggestions offered in this book, can communicate directly with indigenous peoples, alerting us to the rapid appearance of new kinds of relationships and the need to understand what public impact those new relationships will have.

Students and concerned citizens who have entered open debate via various websites[1] have been surprised by their ability to influence areas that were once the exclusive possession of their academic overlords. Whether having the ability to bypass gatekeepers will turn out to be a good thing in the long run remains to be seen, but there is no denying either that the capacity to do this is here to stay or that one of its consequences will be the reining in of our more egregious examples of empathic appropriation.

These new ways of relating are, in conclusion, not at all unproblematic, and they will certainly bring with them all sorts of ethical issues we cannot yet foresee. Will such forms of networking change the face of what we do and how we behave? Almost certainly. Though what will come of this welcome opportunity for involvement remains to be seen, it is clear even to casual observers that the future is a brighter one for those hoping to get involved than it may be for those who have already rubbed repeatedly against Milton's famous spur.

NOTES

1. "Ich will auch nicht mehr ruhen, bis mir nichts mehr Wort und Tradition, sondern lebendiger Begriff ist."

Preface

1. Kant formulated his questions as a natural hierarchy:
1. What can I know? (Epistemology)
2. What should I do? (Ethics)
3. What may I hope? (Religion)
4. What is man? (Anthropology)

2. A version of Chapter 1 was originally published in *American Anthropologist* 96.3 (September 1994). A version of Chapter 2 was originally published in *Exotic No More: Anthropology on the Front Lines* (Chicago 2002); a version of Chapter 3 was originally published in *Contesting Art: Art, Politics and Identity in the Modern World* (Oxford 1997), and an unrevised section of the Epilogue, "No More Einsteins," was originally published in *Le Monde* (*Le Monde diplomatique*, November 2011: 16).

Chapter 2

1. "From extensive pharmacological studies of curare, Norman Bisset at King's College has found that curare carried in calabashes is typically made from species of *Strychnos* [Loganiaceae], whereas curare carried in bamboo tubes is made from *Chondrodendron* [Menispermaceae] or *Curarea* [Menispermaceae]. Unlike the African *Strophanthus* poisons, curare does not affect the heart but instead is a muscle relaxant that kills by paralyzing the muscles required to breathe. Tubocurarine, so named because it was isolated from curare carried in bamboo tubes, and toxiferene, isolated from curare carried in calabashes, have both become crucial anaesthetic drugs for use in surgery; some surgeries, particularly open-heart surgery, would be impossible without these compounds or synthetically modified derivatives" (Balick and Cox 1996, 1997, 118–19).

2. See, for example, Greaves (1994, 6) and Posey (1994, 235). Native Americans have been especially supportive of this position. Richard Deertrack of Taos Pueblo is such an advocate as is Enrique Salmon, a Tarahumara Indian who runs the Baca Institute for Ethnobotany in Crestone, Colorado (personal communication).

3. See, for example, Brown (1998), Conklin and Graham (1995), Kane (1993), and Ramos (1987, 1991, 1994a, 1994b).

4. One may get a taste of this dilemma in a brief and pointed editorial published some years ago in the *Village Voice* (Conason 1986). For a discussion, see Napier (1992).

5. As may be witnessed in the commercially sponsored and oddly romantic *Millennium* television series (see Beidelman 1992).

6. As one would expect, the press has made a feast of Indian resistance and expressions of self-determination. See, for example, *The Economist* (1993). The Kayapó, because of their commercial connections, were among those most heavily criticized for their spending.

7. That is, peoples who have few if any rights that derive from the laws of the countries within the borders of which they may live.

8. This was the United Nations Conference on Environment and Development (UNCED, or Earth Summit) held in Rio de Janeiro in June 1992, out of which came the Rio Declaration, the Convention on Biodiversity, and Agenda 21, in particular, which concerns indigenous knowledge and sustainable development. For a discussion, see Posey (1994).

9. For a summary of these initiatives, see, for instance, Colchester (1994), Cunningham (1992), and Posey (1994).

10. A fact made so glaringly obvious by riots during meetings of the World Trade Organization and by such actions as the Clinton administration's elimination of human rights as a criterion for most favored nation trading status for China.

11. For the later permutation of this document, see Posey (1994, Appendix A).

12. And, yes, alas, these were the same rain forest crunchers who had been applying their profits in ways that appeared alarmingly exploitative—especially to the Body Shop, which found itself in the uneasy position of having to defend activities it might otherwise have found objectionable.

13. To see what the most active monitoring organization advocates, see http://www.rafi.org.

14. For a discussion, see Napier (1986: 43).

15. A "man named Nemo," a Mr. No One, an embodied nothing.

16. "If we're going to grant standing to fictitious entities, we could make the law a more reliable protector of everyone's long-range interests by opening the courthouse doors to the salmon and the sequoia" (Pope 1996: 14).

17. See Roland Marchand's *Creating the Corporate Soul: The Rise of Public Relations and Corporate Imagery in American Big Business* (1998).

18. This shifting identity is most apparent in the recent debates over what the claim "Made in America" actually is allowed to mean. Can, for instance, corporations that manufacture products abroad (e.g., shoes, car parts, electronics) and then assemble them locally actually claim to be making them at home?

19. Though I have written elsewhere about this problem (Napier 1994, 1997), thorough examination of this double bind may be found, for example, in Moustakas (1989) and Strathern (1999).

20. On the complexities of so doing, see Napier (1997). One might also do well to view any of the ethnographic films that focus on this problem (e.g., the films *N!ai*, or *Broken Rainbow*).

21. The catalyst for Benthall's (1999) editorial was an article in the *Times* that warned corporations against being sued by irate shareholders who felt that the companies they invested in had not moved aggressively enough in beating the competition.

22. Though a discussion of mnemonic systems and indigenous forms of mapping boundaries is beyond the scope of this chapter, an examination of the magisterial work of Woodward and Lewis (1998) or Thrower's thought-provoking study (1999) will provide some intimation of the complexities of adjusting modern concepts of property ownership to traditional forms of controlling access to land. For fascinating accounts of aboriginal systems, see, for example, Mowaljarlai and Malnic (1993) and Rose (1992). On the colonial mapping of aboriginal lands, see Ryan (1996).

23. The distinction between copyright and patent is more dramatic than one might at first suspect. In the early 1990s, for instance, Craig Venter, then a scientist at the National Institutes of Health (NIH), intended to use patents to control the rights to new genetic "tags" that he and his colleagues had been identifying "at the rate of 50 to 150 per day" (Hubbard and Wald 1997, 125): "Bernadine Healy, the director of the NIH, says that, although the sequence tags are now meaningless pieces of DNA, the NIH had to seek patents in order to be able to publish the sequences without them falling into the public domain.... Opponents, even within the biotechnology industry, say that, on the contrary, patenting at this stage is likely to limit both scientific and entrepreneurial interest" (ibid.). As Hubbard and Wald point out, the arguments are over the impact of patenting on the protection of ideas, not over issues of morality: "No one here is fighting for the purity of research, or insisting that scientists avoid commercial entanglements" (ibid.).

24. Can an American patent an ancient tree byproduct (Neem) used in India to clean teeth or the aquatic resources of a national park (Yellowstone) simply because no one has yet done so? No, not if it is a natural product; but let the patent applicant secure rights to its efficacious molecules, and control over any byproducts (even to the detriment of those who formerly marketed such byproducts) can be obtained.

25. Which is exceedingly unlikely given the fact that most university researchers can't identify what constitutes a patent.

26. See, for example, Benko (1987) and Brownlie (1992).

27. One such clan was the Menapiers, from which I am happy to have been provided a surname!

28. In America, the hideous levels of political "sponsorship" is evidenced, for instance, in the fact that on average a U.S. senator must make more than $10,000 per day to refinance his or her next election. Is it any wonder that incumbents are so rarely defeated in any election year? The favored method of earning these funds comes from honoraria for so-called speeches given over breakfast with those seeking favors.

29. This is why Amazonian advocates have long campaigned for indigenous parklands. For an excellent argument for advocacy, see, for instance, Colchester (1994); for a polemically described disaster story, see Kane (1993),

30. Even in relatively peaceful Vermont, former Abenaki leader Homer Saint Francis once found himself surrounded by armed police for driving around in a car registered under his homemade tribal license!

31. Though the Human Genome Diversity Project has endorsed the collection of genetic information from the blood of some 722 populations, the fact that this is meant to uncover valuable genetic information that "must lie hidden within such unexplored

genomes" (Hubbard and Wald 1997, 177) has led to justified suspicion and fear among indigenous populations. Indeed, the absence of any moral catalyst for this initiative has led to its being dubbed the Vampire Project (ibid.).

32. These include the World Bank, the United Nations (and its branches the United Nations Development Programme, the United Nations Educational, Scientific and Cultural Organization, the World Health Organization, and the United Nations Economic Commission for Africa) and the following nongovernmental organizations: "1. CIRAN/ Nuffic. Centre for International Research and Advisory Networks, part of the Netherlands Organization for International Cooperation in Higher Education…which publishes the Indigenous Knowledge Systems Monitor. 2. CISDA. Centre for Information Society Development in Africa….3. IDRC. International Development Research Centre….4. ITU. International Telecommunications Union….5. SANGONet. Southern Africa's Nonprofit Internet Service Provider….6. WIPO. World International Property Organization" (Green 1999, 20).

33. For reasons that have more to do with the nature of bench science than the subject of this chapter, it is not surprising that scientists have come very late to the notion that plants, like other molecular organisms, are sometimes like factories and sometimes like people: like factories in the sense that they go through regular cycles of productivity and inactivity; like people in that they are often no less diverse within their respective species than we are in ours.

34. Drug giant Lilly had, for instance, invested millions in Shaman, which it presumably intended not to lose. Shaman fought to forestall collapse through the introduction of new products marketed by its main operating division, ShamanBotanicals. com.

35. For a comparable and rather more famous case, see Napier (1997).

36. Examples of those who have feet planted in more than one world are rare. Few individuals can; for instance, Everett R. Rhodes, MD, functions both as an indigenous healer and director of the Indian Health Service (Rhoades 1996).

Chapter 3

1. Sign above the entrance to a Bureau of Indian Affairs school (Danay in Highwater 1985: 242).

2. In the midst of so many disputes about stolen heritage and repatriation (http:// libguides.stanford.edu/content.php?pid=99699&sid=782780   http://www.repatriation-foundation.org/), it is worth remembering that indigenous peoples have sometimes enthusiastically embraced the sale of traditional objects. Certain West African tribal groups have, for instance, maintained American warehouses of old objects that are periodically sold on the open market. Not all old pieces that appear for sale are, as it often assumed, recently stolen.

3. Here it is worth noting the musing of journalists some years ago at the extravagant Alexander the Great Exhibition at the National Gallery in Washington, D.C., and, in particular, their concern over Alexander, the Macedonian who would never have been thought a Greek by any Athenian of his day.

4. See, for example, Geertz (1964).

5. For discussion, see Napier (1992: 51–76).

6. I remember once attending a Survival International symposium at which an indigenous spokesman for an Amazonian rainforest coalition at once condemned clear-cutting as destructive while advocating traditional slash-and-burn (swidden) gardening methods whereby the forest is set on fire to clear it.

7. Barth's well-known idea of culture as an empty vehicle is worth recalling here. According to this concept, culture is defined by liminal individuals who reside at its periphery—that is, on the borders between the village and the bush where it is constantly being negotiated.

8. Once the organic view of culture (pioneered by Émile Durkheim and named by Wallace) is replaced with the aforementioned model of peripheral contestation, the roles of liminal individuals and the conflicts that arise around them become central to understanding human responses to what is normative. In Western (i.e., Greek) civilization this role is embodied in the figure of the *mangas* (cf. Malampas)—one who, at once, disrupts social unity but in so doing becomes its measure.

9. The concept of Protestant Buddhism is described in Gombrich's *Theravāda Buddhism* (2006 [1988]).

10. For an actual sense of how disjunctive these economic realities may be, see, for example, the film *Cannibal Tours*.

11. In many cultures the idea of a moral economy would be taken as an oxymoron.

12. Here, a rhetoric of cultural difference can only obfuscate the ways Christian and Papuan ideas were actually similar. This problem is elsewhere seen in contemporary politically correct discourse on cultural pluralism—in, as it were, the potluck dinner view of culture (where everyone brings a different dish but behaves by the same old rules; see Napier 2003). I even recently heard an African American speaking nostalgically about a lost ghetto cohesion and communality—one that was actually intensified by the pressures of racial segregation. These are all what I would call autoimmunological reactions—that is, reactions where the self turns inward due to the absence of a defining other. See, for example, Ricoeur's *Oneself as Another* (1992 [1990]).

13. On consumption, attachment, and materiality, see in particular the works of Daniel Miller (e.g., 2001, 2008).

14. The loan office of one of England's largest banks now refuses to offer favorable rates to companies that are not green. The argument is not that those who misbehave don't deserve money, but that any company that is not enough aware of the need to behave in a politically correct fashion is unlikely to survive long enough to repay its debts.

Postscript

1. See, for example, Public Anthropology (http://www.publicanthropology.org) or the Network for Student Activism (http://www.ucl.ac.uk/applied-global-citizenship/network-student-activism).

BIBLIOGRAPHY

Abram, David (1984–85). "Sleight of Hand." *Appalachia*, Winter: 10–21.

Appadurai, Arjun (ed) (1988). *The Social Life of Things: Commodities in Cultural Perspective*. Cambridge: Cambridge University Press.

Armstrong, Robert Plant (1971). *The Affecting Presence: An Essay in Humanistic Anthropology*. Urbana: University of Illinois Press.

Balick, Michael J., and Cox, Paul A. (1997). *Plants, People, and Culture: The Science of Ethnobotany*. New York: Scientific American Library.

Beidelman, Thomas. O. (1992). "Millennium: Tribal Wisdom and the Modern World" (Review Article), *Cultural Anthropology* 7: 508–15.

Bell, Catherine (ed) (2007). *Teaching Ritual*. New York: Oxford University Press.

——. (2009)a *Ritual: Perspectives and Dimensions*. Rev. ed. New York: Oxford University Press.

——. (2009)b *Ritual Theory, Ritual Practice*. New York: Oxford University Press.

Benko, Robert P. (1987). *Protecting Intellectual Property Rights: Issues and Controversies*. Washington, DC: American Enterprise Institute for Public Policy Research.

Benthall, Jonathan (1999). "The Critique of Intellectual Property." *Anthropology Today* 15: 1–3.

Berger, Louis (2006). *The Unboundaried Self: Putting the Person Back into the View from Nowhere*. Victoria, BC: Trafford Publishing.

Bisset, Norman G. (1991). "One Man's Poison, Another Man's Medicine?" *Journal of Ethnopharmacology* 32: 71–81.

Borofsky, Robert (2005). *Yanomami: The Fierce Controversy and What We Can Learn from It*. Berkeley: University of California Press.

Bourdieu, Pierre (1977 [1972]). *Outline of a Theory of Practice*. Trans. Richard Nice. Cambridge: Cambridge University Press.

Brown, Michael F. (1998). "Can Culture Be Copyrighted?" *Current Anthropology* 19: 193–222.

Brownlie, Ian (1992). *Treaties and Indigenous Peoples: The Robb Lectures, 1991*. Oxford: Oxford University Press.

Brush, Stephen B., and Stabinsky, Doreen (eds) (1996). *Valuing Local Knowledge: Indigenous Peoples and Intellectual Property Rights*. Washington, DC: Island Press.

Burton, Thomas M. (1994). "Magic Bullets: Drug Company Looks to 'Witch Doctors' to Conjure Products." *Wall Street Journal*, July 7, 1, 8.

Butler, Judith (1989). "Foucault and the Paradox of Bodily Inscriptions." *Journal of Philosophy* 86: 601–7.

Clifton, James A. (ed) (1990). *The Invented Indian: Cultural Fictions and Government Policies*. New Brunswick, NJ: Transaction Publishers.

Cohen, Lawrence (1998). *No Aging in India. Alzheimer's, the Bad Family, and Other Modern Things*. Berkeley: University of California Press.

Colchester, Marcus (1994). *Salvaging Nature: Indigenous Peoples, Protected Areas and Biodiversity Conservation*. Discussion Paper. Geneva: Diane Publishing.

Conason, Joe (1986). "Homeless on the Range: Greed, Religion, and the Hopi-Navajo Land Dispute." *Village Voice*, July 29, 19–26, 73.

Conklin, Beth A. and Graham, Laura R. (1995). "The Shifting Middle Ground: Amazonian Indians and Eco-Politics." *American Anthropologist* 97: 695–710.

Coombe, Rosemary J. (1993). "The Properties of Culture and the Politics of Possessing Identity: Native Claims in the Cultural Appropriation Controversy." *Canadian Journal of Law and Jurisprudence* 6: 249–84.

—— (1998)a. "Intellectual Property, Human Rights and Sovereignty: New Dilemmas in International Law Posed by the Recognition of Indigenous Knowledge and the Conservation of Biodiversity." *Indiana Journal of Global Legal Studies* 6: 59–115.

—— (1998)b. *The Cultural Life of Intellectual Properties: Authorship, Appropriation, and the Law*. Durham, NC: Duke University Press.

Corry, Stephen (1993). *Harvest Moonshine Taking You for a Ride*. London: Survival International.

Csordas, Thomas (1994). *The Sacred Self: A Cultural Phenomenology of Charismatic Healing*. Berkeley: University of California Press.

—— (2002). *Body/Mind/Healing*. New York: Palgrave Macmillan.

Cunningham, Anthony (1992). *Ethics, Ethnobiological Research, and Biodiversity*. Gland, Switzerland: WWF-World Wide Fund For Nature (formerly World Wildlife Fund).

Danforth, Loring (1989). *Firewalking and Religious Healing: The Anastenaria of Greece and the American Firewalking Movement*. Princeton: Princeton University Press.

de Certeau, Michel (1984). *The Practice of Everyday Life*. Trans. Steven Rendall. Berkeley: University of California Press.

Deren, Maya (1953). *Divine Horsemen: The Living Gods of Haiti*. London: Thames and Hudson.

Doniger, Wendy (2009). *The Hindus: An Alternative History*. New York: Penguin.

Douglas, Mary (1966). *Purity and Danger: An Analysis of Concepts of Pollution and Taboo*. London: Routledge.

Durkheim, Émile (2008) [1912]. *The Elementary Forms of Religious Life*. Oxford: Oxford Paperbacks.

The Economist (1993). "The Savage Can Also Be Ignoble." June 12, 76.

Ellen, Roy (ed) (2006). *Ethnobiology and the Science of Humankind*. Journal of the Royal Anthropological Institute Special Issue Book. Oxford: Blackwell.

Endo, Shusaku (1969). *Silence*. Trans. William Johnston. Rutland, VT: Tuttle.

Finucane, Ronald C. (1977). *Miracles and Pilgrims: Popular Beliefs in Medieval England*. London: Rowman and Littlefield.

Fischer, Michael M. J. (2004). *Emergent Forms of Life and the Anthropological Voice.* Durham, NC: Duke University Press

Florio, Maria and Mudd, Victor (1986). *Broken Rainbow* (70 min. [film/video]). Directed by Victor Mudd and Thom Tyson. Earthworks/Direct Cinema.

Forgacs, David (ed) (1988). *An Antonio Gramsci Reader: Selected Writings, 1916–1935.* New York: Schocken Books.

Freud, Sigmund, and Breuer, Josef (1974) [1895]. *Studies on Hysteria.* London: Penguin.

Geertz, Clifford (1964). "Internal Conversion in Contemporary Bali." In *Malayan and Indonesian Studies Presented to Sir Richard Winstedt*, ed. J. Bastin and R. Roolvink, Oxford.

Gell, Alfred (1998). *Art and Agency: An Anthropological Theory.* Oxford: Clarendon Press.

Godelier, Maurice 1999 (1996). *The Enigma of the Gift.* Trans. Nora Scott. Chicago: University of Chicago Press.

Gombrich, Richard F. (2006 [1988]). *Theravāda Buddhism: A Social History from Ancient Benares to Modern Colombo.* 2nd ed. London: Routledge.

Greaves, Tom (ed) (1994). *Intellectual Property Rights for Indigenous Peoples: A Source Book.* Oklahoma City: Society for Applied Anthropology.

Green, Edward C. (1999). "Indigenous Knowledge for Development." *Anthropology News* 40: 20.

Greenfield, Jeanette (1989). *The Return of Cultural Treasures.* Cambridge: Cambridge University Press.

Grimes, Ronald L. (1986). "Desecration of the Dead: An Inter-Religious Controversy." *American Indian Quarterly* 10: 305–18.

——— (2000). *Deeply into the Bone: Re-Inventing Rites of Passage.* Life Passages Series, Vol. 1. Berkeley: University of California Press.

——— (2004) "Ritual, Performance, and the Sequestering of Sacred Space." In L. Buj (ed), *Ritual Economies.* Windsor, ON: University of Windsor Humanities Research Group, 149–68.

——— (2006) *Rite out of Place: Ritual, Media, and the Arts.* New York: Oxford University Press.

Hallowell, A. Irving (1955). *Culture and Experience.* Philadelphia: University of Pennsylvania Press.

Harvard Medical School (1990). *Policy on Conflicts of Interest and Commitment.* Boston: Harvard Medical School.

Harvard University (1988). *Office of Sponsored Research: Principal Investigator's Handbook.* Cambridge, MA: Harvard University. Office for Sponsored Research.

Hecht, David and Maliqalim, Simone (1994). *Invisible Governance: The Art of African Micropolitics.* New York: Autonomedia.

Heidegger, Martin (1962). *Being and Time.* London: SCM Press.

Highwater, Jamake (1985). "Controversy in Native American Art." In E. Wade (ed), *The Arts of the North American Indian: Native Traditions in Evolution.* New York: Hudson Hills Press/Tulsa: Philbrook Arts Centre, 222–42.

Holm, Bill, and Reid, William (1975). *Indian Art of the Northwest Coast.* Seattle: Institute for the Arts, Rice University.

Howes, David (2003). *Sensual Relations: Engaging the Senses in Culture and Social Theory*. Ann Arbor: University of Michigan Press.

——, (ed) (2005). *Empire of the Senses: The Sensual Cultural Reader*. Oxford: Berg.

——, (ed) (2009). *The Sixth Sense Reader*. Oxford: Berg.

Hubbard, Ruth, and Wald, Elijah (1997). *Exploding the Gene Myth: How Genetic Information Is Produced and Manipulated by Scientists, Physicians, Employers, Insurance Companies, Educators, and Law Enforcers*. Boston: Beacon Press.

Humphrey, Caroline, and Hugh-Jones, Stephen (eds) (1992). *Barter, Exchange and Value*. Cambridge: Cambridge University Press.

Humphrey, Nicholas (2002). *The Mind Made Flesh: Frontiers of Psychology and Evolution*. Oxford: Oxford University Press.

Husserl, Edmund (1960) [1931]. *Cartesian Meditations*. Trans. D. Cairns. Dordrecht: Kluwer.

Johnson, Mark (1987). *The Body in the Mind: The Bodily Basis of Meaning, Imagination, and Reason*. Chicago: University of Chicago Press.

Kapferer, Bruce (1997). *The Feast of the Sorcerer: Practices of Consciousness and Power*. Chicago: University of Chicago Press.

Kane, Joe (1993). "With Spears from All Sides." *New Yorker*, September 27, 54–79.

King, Maurice (1990). "Health is a Sustainable State." *The Lancet*, 336: 664–7.

——, et al. (1991). *NU Nytt om U-landshalsovard* 1.

Kleinman, Arthur; Das, Veena, and Lock, Margaret (eds) (1997). *Social Suffering*. Berkeley: University of California Press.

Laing, Ronald David (1960). *The Divided Self: An Existential Study in Sanity and Madness*. Harmondsworth: Penguin.

Lambek, Michael, and Antze, Paul (eds) (2004). *Illness and Irony: On the Ambiguity of Suffering in Culture*. Oxford: Blackwell.

Latour, Bruno, and Peter Weibel (eds) (2002). *Iconoclash: Beyond the Image Wars in Science, Religion, and Art*. Boston: ZIK and MIT Press.

Lawrence, Peter (1964). *Road Belong Cargo*. Manchester: Manchester University Press.

Leach, Edmund R. (1964). "Anthropological Aspects of Language: Animal Categories and Verbal Abuse." In E.H. Lenneberg. (ed), *New Directions in the Study of Language*. Cambridge, MA: MIT Press, 23–63.

—— (1969). *Genesis as Myth and Other Essays*. London: Cape.

—— (1970). *Claude Lévi-Strauss*. New York: Penguin Classics.

Leenhardt, Maurice (1970) [1942]. *La Structure de la personne en Mélanésie*. Milan: S.T.O.A.

——. (1979) [1947]. *Do Kamo: Person and Myth in the Melanesian World*. Trans. Basia Miller Gulati. Chicago: The University of Chicago Press.

Lehrman, Fredric. 1988. *The Sacred Landscape*. Berkeley: University of California Press.

Lévy-Bruhl, Lucien. 1965 [1928 (1927)]. *The Soul of the Primitive*. Trans. Lillian A. Clare. London: Macmillan.

——. 1966 [1926 (1910)]. *How Natives Think*. New York: Washington Square Press.

——. 1975 [1923 (1922)]. *The Notebooks on Primitive Mentality*. New York: Harper and Row.

Lévi-Strauss, Claude (1969) [1949]. *The Elementary Structures of Kinship*. Rodney Needham (ed). Trans. J. H. Bell, J. R. von Sturmer, and Rodney Needham. Boston: Beacon Press.

—— (1987) [1950]. *Introduction to the Work of Marcel Mauss*. Trans. Felicity Baker. London: Routledge & Kegan Paul.

—— (1974) [1955]. *Tristes Tropiques*. Trans. John and Doreen Weightman. New York: Athenaeum.

—— (1972) [1958]. *Structural Anthropology*. Trans. Claire Jacobson and Brooke Grundfest Schoepf. New York: Basic Books.

—— (1966) [1962]. *The Savage Mind*. Chicago: University of Chicago Press.

—— (1963) [1962]. *Totemism*. Trans. Rodney Needham. Boston: Beacon Press.

—— (1978) [1973]. *Structural Anthropology II*. Trans. Monique Layton. London: Penguin.

Lienhardt, Godfrey (1961). *Divinity and Experience: The Religion of the Dinka*. Oxford: Oxford University Press.

MacClancy, Jeremy (1986). "Mana: An Anthropological Metaphor for Island Melanesia." *Oceania* 57, 2: 142–53.

Maine, Sir Henry J.S. (1861). *Ancient Law: Its Connection to the History of Early Society*. London: J. Murray.

Makarius, Laura (1974). *Le Sacré et la violation des interdits*. Paris: Payot.

Malinowski, Bronislaw (1922). *Argonauts of the Western Pacific: An Account of Native Enterprise and Adventure in the Archipelagoes of Melanesian New Guinea*. London: Routledge.

Marchand, Roland (1998). *Creating the Corporate Soul: The Rise of Public Relations and Corporate Imagery in American Big Business*. Berkeley: University of California Press.

Marcus, George E., and Myers, Fred R. (eds) (1995). *The Traffic in Culture: Refiguring Art and Anthropology*. Berkeley: University of California Press.

Marcus, George E., and Fischer, Michael M.J. (1999). *Anthropology as Cultural Critique: An Experimental Moment in the Human Sciences*, 2nd ed. Chicago: University of Chicago Press.

Marshall, John, and Marshall-Cabezas, Sue (1980). *N!ai: The Story of a !Kung Woman* (59 min. [film/video]). Directed and edited by Adrienne Miesmer and John Marshall. Documentary Educational Resources.

Mauss, Marcel (1967)[1923–24]. *The Gift: Forms and Functions of Exchange in Archaic Societies*. New York: W.W. Norton.

—— (1935). "Les Techniques du corps." *Journal de Psychologie normal et pathologique* 32: 271–93.

McBryde, Isabel (ed) (1985). *Who Owns the Past?* Melbourne: Oxford University Press.

McDannell, Colleen (1998). *Material Christianity: Religion and Popular Culture in America*. New Haven, CT: Yale University Press.

Merges, Robert. P., and Nelson, Richard. R. (1990). "On the Complex Economics of Patent Scope." *Columbia Law Review* 90: 839–916.

Merleau-Ponty, Maurice (2005) [1945]. *Phenomenology of Perception*. Trans. Colin Smith. London: Routledge.

Messenger, Phyllis M. (1989). *The Ethics of Collecting Cultural Property: Whose Culture? Whose Property?* Albuquerque: University of New Mexico Press.

Miller, Daniel (2001). *Car Cultures*. Oxford: Berg.

—— (2008). *The Comfort of Things*. Cambridge: Cambridge University Press.

Mitchell, William E. (1996). "Communicating Culture: Margaret Mead and the Practice of Popular Anthropology." In J. MacClancy and C. McDonough (eds) *Popularizing Anthropology*. London: Routledge, 122–34.

Morgan, David (2012). *The Embodied Eye: Religious Visual Culture and the Social Life of Feeling*. Berkeley: University of California Press.

Mountford, Charles P. (1965). *Ayers Rock: Its People, Their Beliefs, and Their Art*. Honolulu: East-West Centre Press.

Moustakas, John (1989). "Group Rights in Cultural Property: Justifying Strict Inalienability." *Cornell Law Review* 74: 1179–227.

Mowaljarlai, David, and Malnic, Jutta (1993). *Yorro, Yorro: Everything Standing Up Alive: Spirit of the Kimberley*. Broome, Western Australia: Magabala Books.

Murray, Stuart (1997). *Rudyard Kipling in Vermont: Birthplace of* The Jungle Books. Bennington, VT: Images From the Past.

Napier, A. David (1986). *Masks, Transformation, and Paradox*. Berkeley: University of California Press.

—— (1992). *Foreign Bodies: Performance, Art, and Symbolic Anthropology*. Berkeley: University of California Press.

—— 1994). "Saving or Enslaving: The Paradox of Intellectual Property." *Journal of the Anthropological Society of Oxford* 25: 49–58.

—— (1997). "Losing One's Marbles: Cultural Property and Indigenous Thought." In Jeremy MacClancy (ed), *Contesting Art: Art, Politics and Identity in the Modern World*. Oxford: Berg, 165–82.

—— (2003). *The Age of Immunology: Conceiving a Future in an Alienating World*. Chicago: University of Chicago Press.

—— (2004)a. "Public Anthropology and the Fall of the House of Ushers." *Anthropology News*, September, 6–7.

—— (2004)b. *The Righting of Passage: Perceptions of Change after Modernity*. Philadelphia: University of Pennsylvania Press.

Needham, Rodney (1972). *Belief, Language, and Experience*. Chicago: University of Chicago Press.

Nichols, Bill (1981). *Ideology and the Image: Social Representation in the Cinema and Other Media*. Bloomington: Indiana University Press.

Parker, Eugene (1992). "Forest Islands and Kayapó Resource Management: A Reappraisal of the Apêtê." *American Anthropologist* 92: 406–28.

—— (1993). "Fact and Fiction in Amazonia: The Case of the Apêtê." *American Anthropologist* 93: 715–23.

Parry, Jonathan P., and Bloch, Maurice (eds) (1989). *Money and the Morality of Exchange*. Cambridge: Cambridge University Press.

Payer, Cheryl (1991). *Lent and Lost: Foreign Credit and Third World Development*. London: Zed Books.

Pennebaker, James W. (2003). "Telling Stories: The Health Benefits of Disclosure." In J.M. Wilce Jr. (ed), *Social and Cultural Lives of Immune Systems*. London: Routledge.

Perkins, Harold (1999). "Soul Food for the Boardroom." *Times Literary Supplement* 4999 (January 22): 6.

Pfeiffer, James (2002). "International NGOs and Primary Health Care in Mozambique: The Need for a New Model of Collaboration." *Social Science and Medicine* 56: 725–38.

Pink, Sarah (2009). *Doing Sensory Ethnography*. London: Sage.

Pope, Carl (1996). "Corporate Citizens." *Sierra* 8: 14.

Posey, Darrell A. (1990). "Intellectual Property Rights, and Just Compensation for Indigenous Knowledge." *Anthropology Today* 6: 13–16.

—— (1994). "International Agreements and Intellectual Property Right Protection for Indigenous Peoples." In T. Greaves (ed), *Intellectual Property Rights for Indigenous Peoples: A Source Book*. Oklahoma City, OK: Society for Applied Anthropology, 19–34.

—— (1996). *Traditional Resource Rights: International Instruments for Protection and Compensation for Indigenous Peoples and Local Communities*. Gland, Switzerland: WWF-World Wide Fund For Nature (formerly World Wildlife Fund).

Ramos, Alcida R. (1987). "Reflecting on the Yanomami: Ethnographic Images and the Pursuit of the Exotic." *Cultural Anthropology* 2: 284–304.

—— (1988). "Indian Voices: Contact Experienced and Expressed." In J. Hill (ed) *Rethinking History and Myth: Indigenous South American Perspectives on the Past*. Urbana: University of Illinois Press, 214–34.

—— (1991). "A Hall of Mirrors: The Rhetoric of Indigenism in Brazil." *Critique of Anthropology* 11(2): 155–69.

—— (1994)a. "From Eden to Limbo: The Construction of Indigenism in Brazil." In G. C. Bond and A. Gilliam (eds), *Social Construction of the Past: Representation as Power*, London: Routledge, 29–43.

——.(1994)b. "The Hyperreal Indian." *Critique of Anthropology* 14: 153–71.

Rhoades, Everett R. (1996). "Two Paths to Healing: Can Tradition and Western Scientific Medicine Work Together?" *Winds of Change, American Indian Education and Opportunity* 11: 48–51.

Ricoeur, Paul (1992 [1990]). *Oneself as Another*. Trans. Kathleen Blamey. Chicago: University of Chicago Press.

"Ritual" (2011) Material Religion: The Journal of Objects, Art and Belief. Special issue: Key Words in Material Religion. 7.1: 77–83.

River, William. H. R. 2001 [1924]. *Magic, Medicine, and Religion*. London: Routledge.

Rose, Deborah B. (1992). *Dingo Makes Us Human: Life and Land in an Aboriginal Australian Culture*. Cambridge: Cambridge University Press.

Rothenberg, Albert (1988). "Creativity and the Homospatial Process: Experimental Studies." *Psychiatric Clinics of North America* 11: 443–59.

Ryan, Simon (1996). *The Cartographic Eye: How Explorers Saw Australia*. Cambridge: Cambridge University Press.

Sax, William; Quack, Johannes, and Weinhold, Jan (eds) 2010. *The Problem of Ritual Efficacy*. New York: Oxford University Press.

Schechner, Richard (1993). *The Future of Ritual: Writings on Culture and Performance*. London: Routledge.

Scheper-Hughes, Nancy, and Wacquant, Loïc (eds) (2002). *Commodifying Bodies*. London: Sage.

Scott, James C. (1985). *Weapons of the Weak: Everyday Forms of Peasant Resistance*. New Haven: Yale University Press.

—— (2009). *The Art of Not Being Governed: An Anarchist History of Southeast Asia*. New Haven: Yale University Press.

Sillitoe, Paul (1998). "The Development of Indigenous Knowledge: A New Applied Anthropology." *Current Anthropology* 19: 223–52.

Sioui, Georges E. (1992). *For an Amerindian Autohistory: An Essay on the Foundations of a Social Ethic*. Trans. Sheila Fischman. Montreal: McGill-Queens University Press.

Sittenfeld, Ana, and Gamez, Rodrigo (1993). "Biodiversity Prospecting by INBio." In W.V. Reid et al. (eds), *Biodiversity Prospecting: Using Genetic Resources for Sustainable Development*. Washington, DC: Word Resources Institute, 69–97.

Skidelsy, Robert (2009). *Keynes: The Return of the Master*. New York: Allen Lane.

Smith, Jonathan Z. (1987). *To Take Place: Toward Theory in Ritual*. Chicago: University of Chicago Press.

—— (2004). *Relating Religion: Essays in the Study of Religion*. Chicago: University of Chicago Press.

Srinivas, Krishna R. (2012). "Protecting Traditional Knowledge Holders' Interests and Preventing Misappropriation—Traditional Knowledge Commons and Biocultural Protocols: Necessary but Not Sufficient?" *International Journal of Cultural Property* 19: 401–22.

Starn, Orin (2004). *Ishi's Brain: In Search of America's Last "Wild" Indian*. New York: W.W. Norton.

Stephenson, Barry (2010). *Performing the Reformation: Public Ritual in the City of Luther*. New York: Oxford University Press.

Stoll, David (1995). "Guatemala: Solidarity Activists Head for Trouble." *Christian Century*, January 4–11, 17–21.

Stoller, Paul (1989)a. *Fusion of the Worlds: An Ethnography of Possession among the Songhay of Niger*. Chicago: University of Chicago Press.

Stoller, Paul (1989)b. *The Taste of Ethnographic Things: The Senses in Anthropology*. Philadelphia: University of Pennsylvania Press.

—— (1997). *Sensuous Scholarship*. Philadelphia: University of Pennsylvania Press.

—— (2002). *Money Has No Smell: The Africanization of New York City*. Chicago: University of Chicago Press.

Stoller, Paul, and Olkes, Cheryl (1989). *In Sorcery's Shadow: A Memoire of Apprenticeship among the Songhay of Niger*. Chicago: University of Chicago Press.

Strathern, Marilyn (1988). *The Gender of the Gift: Problems with Women and Problems with Society in Melanesia*. Berkeley: University of California Press.

—— (1999). *Property, Substance and Effect: Anthropological Essays on Persons and Things*. London: Athlone Press.

Suchman, Mark. C. (1989). "Invention and Ritual: Notes on the Interrelation of Magic and Intellectual Property in Preliterate Societies." *Columbia Law Review* 89: 1264–94.

Tauber, Alfred I. (ed) (1991). *Organism and the Origins of the Self*. Boston Studies in the Philosophy of Science, Vol. 129. Dordrecht: Kluwer.

Thrower, Norman J. W. (1999). *Maps & Civilization: Cartography in Culture and Society*, 2nd ed. Chicago: University of Chicago Press.

Tuan, Yi-fu (1974). *Topophilia: A Study of Environmental Perception, Attitudes, and Values*. New York: Columbia University Press.

Tuan, Yi-fu and Hoelscher Tuan, Steven (2001). *Space and Place: The Perspective of Experience*. Minneapolis: University of Minnesota Press.

Turner, Terence (1991). "Representing, Resisting, Rethinking: Historical Transformations of Kayapó Culture and Anthropological Consciousness." In G. Stocking (ed)

Colonial Situations: Essays on the Contextualization of Ethnographic Knowledge. Madison: University of Wisconsin Press, 285–313.

—— (1992). "Defiant Images: The Kayapó Appropriation of Video." *Anthropology Today* 8: 5–16.

—— (1993). "The Role of Indigenous peoples in the Environmental Crisis: The Example of the Kayapó of the Brazilian Amazon." *Perspectives in Biology and Medicine* 36: 526–45.

Turner, Victor (1975). *Dramas, Fields, and Metaphors: Symbolic Action in Human Society*. Ithaca, NY: Cornell University Press.

—— (1988). *The Anthropology of Performance*. New York: PAJ Books.

—— (2001). *From Ritual to Theatre: The Human Seriousness of Play*. New York: Performing Arts Journal.

Tylor, Sir Edward B. (1913) [1871]. *Primitive Culture: Researches into the Development of Mythology, Philosophy, Religion, Language, Art, and Custom*. 2 vols. London: John Murray.

van Gennep, Arnold. (1960) [1909]. *The Rites of Passage*. Chicago: University of Chicago Press.

Vidal, Gore (1988). *At Home: Essays 1982–88*. New York: Random House.

Warde, Ibrahim (2011). "Higher Finance." *Le Monde diplomatique*, September, 4–5.

Weiner, Annette B. (1985). "Inalienable Wealth." *American Ethnologist* 12: 52–65.

—— (1992). *Inalienable Possessions: The Paradox of Keeping-While-Giving*. Berkeley: University of California Press.

Whorf, Benjamin Lee. 1997 [1956]. *Language, Thought, and Reality: Selected Writings of Benjamin Lee Whorf*. Ed. John B. Carroll. Cambridge, MA: MIT Press.

Wikan, Unni. 1990. *Managing Turbulent Hearts: A Balinese Formula for Living*. Chicago: University of Chicago Press.

Woodmansee, Martha (1994). *The Author, Art, and the Market: Rereading the History of Aesthetics*. New York: Columbia University Press.

Woodward, David, and Lewis, G. Malcolm (eds) (1998). *The History of Cartography, Volume Two, Book Three: Cartography in the Traditional African, American, Artic, Australian, and Pacific Societies*. Chicago: University of Chicago Press.

Worsley, Peter (1968). *The Trumpet Shall Sound: A Study of "Cargo" Cults in Melanesia*, 2nd ed. London: Macgibbon & Kee.

Wright, Robin (1988). "Anthropological Presuppositions of Indigenous Advocacy." *Annual Review of Anthropology* 17: 365–90.

Counter-Reformation, 122, 129
Corry, S., 57, 58
cosmology, 1–4, 12, 28–29, 33–34,
    93–95, 106–109, 157
creativity, x–xiii, 25, 61, 71, 79–83,
    113–115, 118–123, 137–141,
    143–145, 148–153
Csordas, T., 2, 118
culture
    cultural property rights (*see* Rights)
    cultural values, x, 6–8, 47–50, 56,
        65, 70, 86–88, 92, 96–97, 99–102,
        131–133, 137

Dali, S., 136, 143
Danforth, L., 4
Das, V., 12
de Certeau, M., 4
de Bono, E., 150
Deertrack, R., 161n2
Deren, M., 51
Dionne, P., 147
Divination, 16, 119
Doniger, W., 105
Douglas, M., 3
dreams, 2, 23, 66, 109–110, 121, 136
Durkheim, E., 3, 117, 165n8
Deertrack, R., 161n2
Deren, M., 51
Dionne, P., 147
Divination, 16, 119
Doniger, W., 105
Douglas, M., 3
dreams, 2, 23, 66, 109–110, 121, 136
Durkheim, E., 3, 117, 165n8

economics, xiv, 3, 6, 9, 11–12, 29–31,
    42, 55, 57–58, 68, 70–73, 83, 93,
    99–101, 133, 152–153, 165n10
Edison, T., 132, 151
Einstein, A., 149, 152
Empiricism, 110–111, 119
Endo, S., 61
Enlightenment, x–xi, 5, 133–134
Ensor, J., 137
environmental behavior, 2, 15–20, 26–28,
    47–49, 53, 74–75, 79–81, 86, 91, 97,
    105–110, 113–114, 116, 118–121,
    125–126, 132–134
exchange, xiv, 6–10, 30, 42, 59, 79–102,
    105–109, 111, 121–125, 128–129
experience, x, 1–4, 12, 16–20, 22–23, 25,
    31–32, 47–49, 53–54, 79–81, 86, 90,
    97, 109–111, 114, 118, 121–122,
    126, 134–136, 143, 155–157

fanon, 69, 115
fetish, 4, 18, 22, 26–27, 30, 96–97, 110,
    120–121, 132, 140
Finucane, R., 2
Fischer, M., 154
Ford, H., 132
Forgacs, D., 69
Foucault, M., 114
Freud, S., 27, 30, 110, 119–121
Fuente, L., 28

Gamez, R., 72
Gardner, R., 147
Gell, A., xiv
globalization, 2, 6–9, 12, 19, 28–30,
    42, 52, 55, 57, 74, 99, 101–102,
    107, 114–115, 124–125, 128–130,
    140, 152
Godelier, M., xiv
Goethe, J.W., vi
Gorinski, C., 67
Greaves, T., 70, 161n2
Greenspan, A., 61
Grimes, R., 2, 4

Hallowell, A.I., 3
Hecht, D., 95, 112
Hegel, G.W.F., 6
hegemony, 9, 12, 69–71, 112, 115
Heidegger, M., 111, 120
heritage, 6, 53, 64–65, 84–85, 164n2
Hesse, H., 149–150
Highwater, J., 85
Holm, B., 87–88
Howes, D., 4
Humphrey, N., 116–118
Husserl, E., 111, 137
Huxley, F., 145, 148